A Photo Gallery

CITY TRANSIT BUSES
of the 20th Century

William A. Luke and Linda L. Metler

Iconografix

Iconografix
PO Box 446
Hudson, Wisconsin 54016 USA

The information in this book is true and complete to the best of our knowledge. All recommendations are made without any guarantee on the part of the author or Publisher, who also disclaim any liability incurred in connection with the use of this data or specific details.

We acknowledge that certain words, such as model names and designations, mentioned herein are the property of the trademark holder. We use them for purposes of identification only. This is not an official publication.

Iconografix books are offered at a discount when sold in quantity for promotional use. Businesses or organizations seeking details should write to the Marketing Department, Iconografix, at the above address.

Library of Congress Control Number: 2005927238

ISBN-13: 978-1-58388-146-0
ISBN10: 1-58388-146-8

05 06 07 08 09 10 6 5 4 3 2 1

Printed in China

Cover and book design by Dan Perry

Copyedited by Suzie Helberg

On the cover: Top left, see page 22
Top center, see page 94
Top right, see page 150
Main image, see page 122

Book Proposals

Iconografix is a publishing company specializing in books for transportation enthusiasts. We publish in a number of different areas, including Automobiles, Auto Racing, Buses, Construction Equipment, Emergency Equipment, Farming Equipment, Railroads & Trucks. The Iconografix imprint is constantly growing and expanding into new subject areas.

Authors, editors, and knowledgeable enthusiasts in the field of transportation history are invited to contact the Editorial Department at Iconografix, Inc., PO Box 446, Hudson, WI 54016.

Table of Contents:

About the Authors

William A. (Bill) Luke has been involved in the bus transportation industry his entire life, both personally and professionally. Raised in northern Minnesota, he began his career with Minneapolis-based Jefferson Transportation Company. He remained with Jefferson for more than 20 years, serving in a variety of positions, including schedule director and assistant secretary. He left Jefferson in 1969 to become assistant manager of Empire Lines in Spokane, Washington.

With the help of his wife, Adelene, Bill established *Bus Ride*, which began in 1965 as a mimeographed newsletter and went on to become the premier trade journal of the bus industry. The Lukes incorporated in 1973 as Friendship Publications, Inc. to publish *Bus Ride* and to produce a number of bus industry directories. The company also conducted Bus Maintenance Forums in various locations in the United States.

Although Friendship Publications was sold in 1996, Bill has continued to serve the bus transportation industry. He has been a transit commissioner and member of several transit committees in Spokane. He has travel extensively throughout the United States, Canada and more than 70 countries around the world, visiting, making friends and learning about bus transportation. He established the Buses International Association, a fellowship organization for bus professionals which has members in 22 countries around the world. The American Public Transit Association honored Bill for his years of service to the public transportation industry by inducting him into its Hall of Fame.

Bill and Adelene have been married since 1953 and still live in Spokane. He continues to travel and serves as a consultant and freelance writer. He has written *Bus Industry Chronicle*, a history of the entire bus industry in the United States and Canada. He is also the author or co-author of nine Photo Archive books published by Iconografix, Inc. The books draw on the many photographs, extensive research material and other information Bill has collected in his more than 50 years with the bus industry.

Linda Metler began her association with the bus industry as an employee of Friendship Publications. She served as graphics manager and helped transition the company to desktop publishing. She traveled extensively for the magazine, visiting bus companies and transit agencies in the U.S. and Canada and writing articles from those visits. Her interest in computers has helped in compiling and completing this book.

Linda and her husband, Don, a land surveyor, also live in Spokane. They have two grown daughters and three grandchildren.

Bibliography

2000 *Bus Industry Chronicle* William A. Luke
1988 *The Bus World Encyclopedia of Buses* Ed Stauss
1989 *The Complete Encyclopedia of Commercial Vehicles*
      G. N. Georgano G. Marshal Naul
1965-1996 *Bus Ride* Magazines
1972-1996 *Bus Industry Directory*
Motor Coach Age-various issues
Bus Transportation Magazine-various issues
Iconografix Photo Archive Books-various editions

Acknowledgments

Brenda Borwege, Vice President, ABC Companies, Faribault, Minnesota

Cliff Henke, Acadia, California

Roger Hristovski, Contract Specialist, New Flyer Industries, Winnipeg, Manitoba

Tom Jones, Motor Bus Society, Clark, New Jersey

Steve Kratzer, Marketing and Business Development Representative, Optima Bus Corporation, Valley Center, Kansas

Paul Leger, President, Bus History Association, Halifax, Nova Scotia

Brian Macleod, Senior Vice President, Gillig Corporation, Hayward, California

Peter Newgard, President, Transit Heritage Foundation, Gloucester, Ontario

Introduction

The interesting history of the bus industry in the cities of the United States and Canada is presented in the chapters of this book. Many of the buses built in the past century are pictured, along with descriptions. It has been possible to include many of the popular buses used in city service over the years, but there are many unusual buses as well. Big buses, early double-deck vehicles, and today's common articulated buses are shown. Everything from small buses of the early days to shuttle-type buses used in recent years will be found on the pages of this book. There is also much trivia included.

The revolutionary Twin Coach Model 40 bus, introduced in 1927, is emphasized. There are a number of pictures of this special bus, which lead the way to the future.

Trolley buses, which were important in a number of cities following the demise of streetcars, are pictured, and some modern trolley buses are also included.

This book tells about the great number of bus manufacturers in the market prior to World War II, and the influx of new bus designs by the more traditional manufacturers in the postwar years. Then it describes the big changes in the industry caused by declining city bus patronage and competition among the leading bus manufacturers. This resulted in the end of bus production by most of the large bus builders, some of which had been building buses for 40 to 50 years.

The book goes on to describe the new era in transit that began in the 1960s. Prior to that time private companies operated most city transit systems. Then, as ridership declined, it became necessary for the federal government and other government bodies in the United States to step in to subsidize the transit systems.

The buses of the 21st Century and the future are pictured in the final pages of this book to give readers an idea of what is ahead in the city bus business. There is an emphasis on Bus Rapid Transit and busways, which will be important as city bus systems attempt to increase ridership in today's fast-paced world and economic uncertainties.

Many of the pictures in this book have never been published previously. Information explaining each bus and the bus systems has been obtained from a number of sources. Historical documentation of the buses and bus systems is not always available or, if it is found, is not always complete. Sometimes it is surprising to find interesting facts from new sources.

All attempts have been made to be sure facts and dates are as accurate as possible, but occasionally historical accounts do not agree. Those interested in a more detailed history of the entire bus industry might find *Bus Industry Chronicle*, another book written by William A. Luke, of interest. This and other sources used to obtain information to produce this book are listed in the Bibliography.

The help of many bus industry people, bus historians, and others is much appreciated. Names of these sources are also included in the Bibliography and Acknowledgments. An Index provides names of the buses, bus systems, manufacturers, and other special information.

This book compliments several of the other Photo Archive books on bus history produced by Iconografix in recent years. It also is a companion to the book *Highway Buses of the 20th Century*, also published by Iconografix.

Chapter 1

Double Deckers and Jitneys

Motorized buses, usually open-top double deckers, began appearing on the streets of the main large cities in the United States in the early 1900s. Up to that time city transit relied almost totally on streetcars. Even in the main cities, buses were rare outside of New York City. In smaller cities buses did not begin to appear until after 1910.

Early city buses were homemade bodies on truck chassis. Early internal combustion engines were not powerful enough to transport more than a few passengers at a time. As engines improved, they became capable of powering larger vehicles, making it possible to carry a number of passengers. The first buses, known as omnibuses, had hard rubber tires, which restricted their speed and made for an uncomfortable ride. Pneumatic tires, which were introduced early in the 1900s, provided a smoother ride, but were not commonly used in city bus operations. Pneumatic tires weren't necessary because most cities had hard-surface streets that provided an easier ride. Buses with hard rubber tires were in use for city transit as late as the 1930s.

The Daimler Company of Coventry, England, built bus number 80 of New York's Fifth Avenue Coach Company, in 1915. The company was one of the first bus builders, beginning prior to 1900. Fifth Avenue Coach Company had 12 Daimler buses, like this one, in its early-day fleet. *Motor Bus Society*

The Fifth Avenue Coach Company in New York City was incorporated in 1896. It was the first company to operate city buses in the United States. Early buses in New York were open-top double-deck buses with hard rubber tires. These first buses, introduced between 1905 and 1910, were DeDion vehicles from France or Daimler buses from England. Several of these early buses are seen on Fifth Avenue in this picture.

In 1902, the first bus began regular passenger service on Fifth Avenue in New York City. The bus was operated by the Fifth Avenue Coach Company, which began in 1896. The Fifth Avenue Coach Company operated horse-drawn buses on Fifth Avenue, which operated without rails in the street surface or overhead wires for streetcars.

In 1905, the Fifth Avenue Coach Company acquired 15 French-built DeDion Bouton double-deck buses. This is said to have been the first bus fleet in the United States. The upper decks of the buses were open, a body style similar to earlier horse-drawn buses. This bus fleet brought an end to the operation of horse-drawn buses with similar bodies and styles on Fifth Avenue. In 1918 the owners of the Fifth Avenue Coach Company began the Chicago Motor Bus Company (later renamed the Chicago Motor Coach Company).

Competing with streetcars in many areas were "jitney" bus operations, which generally consisted of passenger vehicles (touring cars), operated by individuals or syndicates on regular routes on city streets. Northern New Jersey was the scene of many jitney operations in the 1915 era, especially in Hudson, Essex, and Passaic counties and in the cities of Newark, Jersey City, and Elizabeth.

The jitneys provided a unique transit service, and many of these independent bus owners, operating one or two buses on specific routes, survived in Newark and other parts of New Jersey throughout the 20th Century. In areas where several bus owners operated on specific streets or routes, bus associations were established. Interestingly, the buses on each of the routes were very individual, representing a variety of makes of buses, each in different liveries.

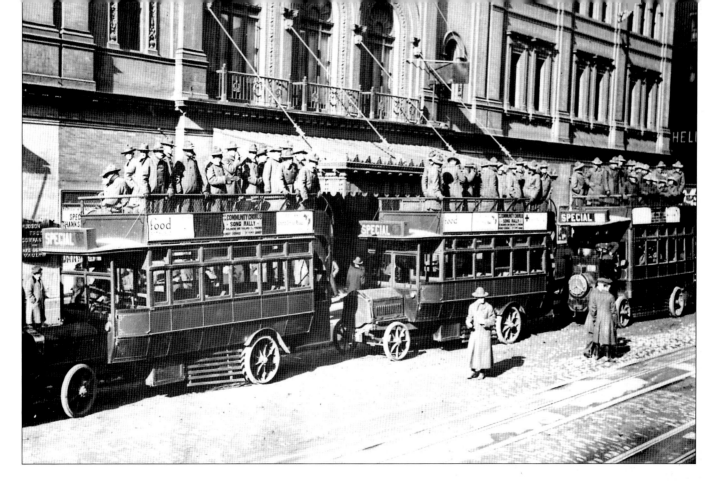

Two Daimler buses and one DeDion double-deck bus of the Fifth Avenue Coach Company are seen in this view of Fifth Avenue in New York City. All the early buses had open-top upper decks. Note the advertising carried on these buses and the interesting guard in front of the rear wheels.

This 1912 French DeDion bus had a Brill body and was one of the many that were in operation in New York City by the Fifth Avenue Coach Company. The driver had a commanding view. Note the bulb horn at the driver's left. Fifth Avenue Coach Company operated 132 DeDion buses.

This French DeDion bus entered service for the Fifth Avenue Coach Company in New York City in 1908. The company operated 20 buses of this type. Originally they had Brill bodies, but later the bodies were rebuilt by Fifth Avenue Coach Company's body-building facility. *Motor Bus Society*

Buses first began to appear in St. Louis, Missouri, in 1915, competing in some cases with the streetcar operator United Railways. A major competitor to United Railways came on the scene in 1923 when Peoples Motor Bus Company was incorporated. One of the first buses operated by Peoples Motor Bus was this 1923 hard-tired double-deck vehicle built by New York's Fifth Avenue Coach Company. Peoples Motor Bus Company stayed in existence for many years before becoming a part of St. Louis Public Service Company, which succeeded United Railways.

Experiments in trolley bus operation were carried out in the early part of the 20th Century. The Field Electric Bus Co. built this trolley bus for the Merrill (Wisconsin) Railway & Lighting Company. This trolley bus went into service in Merrill in 1913, but was discontinued in 1919. The vehicle had hard rubber tires and a somewhat complicated chain drive. The body accommodated 18 passengers. It was a beginning for other trolley bus experiments in the 1920s, which resulted in greater interest in establishing trolley bus services.

The Selden Motor Vehicle Company of Rochester, New York, was established in 1913. Six years later the company was known as the Selden Truck Corporation and built trucks and some buses. This bus operated for the East Avenue Bus Company of Rochester, which was controlled by the New York State Railways, headquartered in Rochester.

Streetcars dominated in most major cities when the first motorbuses began traveling on city streets. Some individuals began operating "jitney" buses in competition with the street railways. Typical of a jitney was this White bus (circa 1915), seen in Kansas City, Missouri, making a stop at 12th and Main Street.

Winnipeg, Manitoba, began urban transportation in 1882. Electric streetcars were introduced in 1891, and the first motorbuses were acquired in 1918. By that time the transit system was known as the Winnipeg Electric Co. The first city buses in Winnipeg were a fleet of four buses on Reo chassis. Buses continued to be added to the fleet.

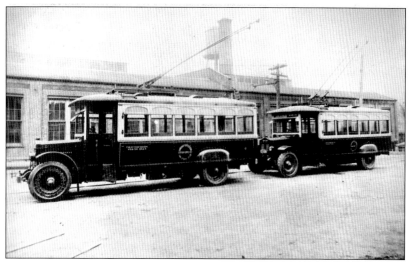

Capital District Transportation Company of Albany, New York, operated one of the earliest trolley bus systems. Capital began a four-vehicle system in suburban Cohoes in 1924. Brockway Corporation of Courtland, New York, built the two trolley buses pictured here. Watson built the bodies. Rochester, New York, also had Brockway trolley buses, but with Kuhlman bodies. The Rochester service ran from 1923 to 1932. The Cohoes service lasted five years longer. The seven trolley buses on these two systems were the only Brockway trolley buses built. The Brockway Co. originated in 1912 and in 1956 became a part of the Mack organization. The Brockway name continued until 1977.

The first bus operated by the Boston (Massachusetts) Elevated Railway was the Republic bus pictured here. Truck building was the main business for its manufacturer, Republic Motor Truck Co., which began in 1913 as Alma Truck Co. of Alma, Michigan. This bus, and others, operated a short route between Boston's Union Square and the North Beacon Street Bridge.

Washington, D.C., had two early bus operating companies, the Washington Rapid Transit Co. and the Washington Railway & Electric Company, beginning in 1921 and 1922, respectively. One of the first buses operated by the Washington Railway & Electric Co. was this 24-passenger White Model 50 bus. White Motor Company of Cleveland, Ohio, was one of the leading bus chassis builders, beginning as early as 1910. *Motor Bus Society*

Toronto (Ontario) Transportation Commission (TTC) began in 1921, which was also when the first city buses began operating in Toronto. In 1922, a company called Veteran in Sherbrooke, Quebec, built a double-deck vehicle, which was one of the first TTC buses.

Fort Madison, Iowa, like many small cities, had a street railway line. It was established in 1895, and replaced mule-drawn cars. The Fort Madison Street Railway Company operated the line. In 1924, this Model AB Mack bus was purchased to supplement the rail service. Note the high-mounted headlights. In April 1930 the Fort Madison streetcars were abandoned. At that time, five Yellow Coach Model U buses were acquired to replace the streetcars. *Mack Museum*

Sioux Falls (South Dakota) Traction Company was one of the streetcar companies that ran buses in its early days. In fact, Sioux Falls Traction Company operated an interstate highway bus service between Sioux Falls and Worthington, Minnesota. This was one of the first buses owned by the Sioux Falls company. It was a White with an Eckland Brothers, Inc. body.

Fifth Avenue Coach Company began building its own buses in 1916. Pictured is one of its open-top double-deck buses. It was built in 1925. Hard rubber tires were still being used, although most buses at the time had pneumatic tires. This picture was taken in 1934, when the bus was still in regular service. *Motor Bus Society*

Seven Yellow Coach Z-C-201, 66-passenger double-deck buses first went into service in 1921 for the Detroit (Michigan) Department of Street Railways. The Department of Street Railways also operated 50 ACF double-deck buses. Detroit's double-deck buses operated primarily on routes such as the John R, the Conant, and the Chalmers, as well as Jefferson Express and Cadillac Express routes.

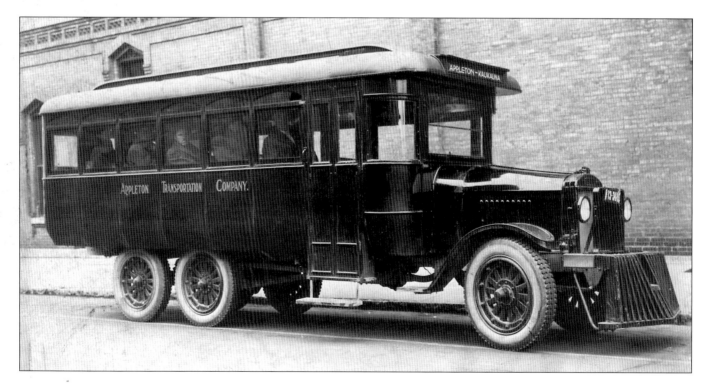

The Appleton Transportation Company operated this interesting bus, a six-wheeled vehicle, in the early 1920s in the Appleton, Wisconsin, area. One of the unique features of the bus was the "cow catcher" in the front. This type of device was common on steam railroad locomotives. It also had a radiator forward of the front of the bus. The make is unknown as well as the year.

Motor City Coach Line, which operated city bus service in one of Michigan's automobile producing cities, had this Model AB bus built by Mack Trucks of Allentown, Pennsylvania. The AB chassis was referred to as a "low bus" chassis. It had a distinctive body and disc wheels. The AB buses were built for both city and intercity service between 1924 and 1937. *Mack Museum*

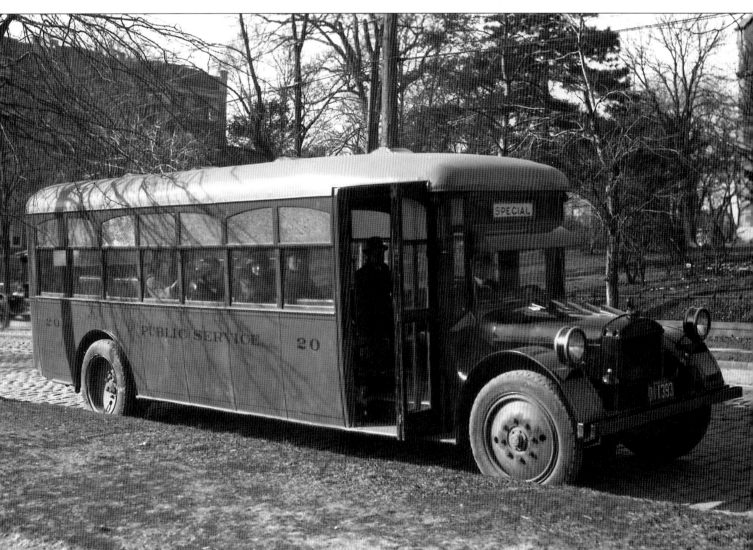

Public Service of New Jersey put two Fageol Safety Coach city buses into service in 1923. Another 25 Fageol Safety Coach chassis were delivered in 1925. The bodies were built in Public Service's New York shops. Public Service had a great variety of bus makes in its fleet until 1926, when Yellow Coach buses became almost exclusive to the New Jersey company. The Fageol Safety Coach was originally designed as an intercity bus and was very popular. However, many versions of the Safety Coach were used in city service in many areas. *Motor Bus Society*

The San Francisco-Oakland Terminal Railways was also known as the Key System in its pioneer days. In 1924 the Key System Transit Company came into being to operate buses in the San Francisco East Bay area. One of its first buses was this Fageol Safety Coach of 1924. The Fageol brothers introduced the revolutionary Safety Coach in 1922. It was primarily for intercity service, but it also became popular as a city bus. The Key System had nine of these buses in its early fleet. *Motor Bus Society*

Fifth Avenue Coach Company of New York City purchased 24 Yellow Coach Model Z-BR-602 chassis in 1931. They were fitted with double-deck bodies with closed upper decks built by Fifth Avenue Coach Company's own body-building facility. The stairway to the upper deck was in the middle of the bus. Seating was for 62 passengers. Although double-deck buses were disappearing from other cities, Fifth Avenue Coach Company continued to add more. *Motor Bus Society*

Philadelphia, Pennsylvania's, transit system operated a fleet of these gas-electric Yellow Coach double-deck buses. In 1938 they received some alterations, including pneumatic tires and fully covered upper decks. Public Service of New Jersey acquired some of these buses in 1929 to operate Pennjersey Rapid Transit routes. Others ran local service in Newark. In the late 1930s the buses were cut down to single-deck units seating 31 passengers.

Public Service of New Jersey began buying Yellow Coach buses soon after Yellow Coach began producing buses. This one, a Model Z-BP-620 seating 38 passengers, was acquired in 1930. This bus and 139 others delivered at about the same time were gas-electric powered. When these buses entered the Public Service fleet the company was operating an extensive transit system throughout New Jersey. *Motor Bus Society*

The United Traction Company operated city bus service in Albany, New York, for many years. It was a subsidiary of the Capital District Transportation Company of Albany. In 1925, a fleet of 19 Fageol gas-electric Safety Coach city buses went into service in the Albany area. Fageol Motors of Ohio in Kent, Ohio, built the buses for Albany.

Chapter 2

The Revolutionary Twin Coach Model 40

The first purpose-built bus in the United States was the Fageol Safety Coach, which was built by brothers Frank R. and William B. Fageol and introduced in 1922. The Safety Coach was designed principally as an intercity bus, but a few city bus operations saw the advantage of its low-gravity type chassis, and some Safety Coaches were used for city bus service.

The Fageol brothers sold their company, Fageol Motors Co., to American Car & Foundry (ACF) of Philadelphia, Pennsylvania. The brothers continued with ACF until starting a new enterprise, The Twin Coach Co., in Kent, Ohio, in 1926.

The Twin Coach Co. introduced a revolutionary bus, the Model 40 Twin Coach. It was the first bus built entirely for city transit use and proved significant to the development of buses for city transit service. In many ways the Twin Coach was very similar to the buses of

The Model 40 Twin Coach opened up new opportunities to city transit properties. The Model 40s were high-capacity buses, with a heavy-duty design, which met the demands of the companies that operated them. This new bus originally had two Waukesha engines mounted on each side of the bus. The Houston (Texas) Electric Company was one of the first companies to use the Model 40 Twin Coach and had 33 in its fleet between 1927 and 1931. Houston had transit service as early as 1874. Buses were in service as early as 1924. *Motor Bus Society*

The Twin Coach Co., of Kent, Ohio, which was founded in 1927 by Frank and William Fageol, introduced a dual-engine bus in 1927. It became known as the Model 40 and was a huge success. More than 1,000 of these buses were built. They were seen in many large cities across the country. Chicago (Illinois) Surface Lines was the first company to purchase these Twin Coach buses and operated 10 of them. *George Krambles Archive*

today. It could be called the grandfather of the modern transit bus.

The Model 40 was the first high-capacity city bus, carrying 40 passengers. The entrance door was ahead of the front wheels, a first for a bus. Unlike previous buses, which had the engine in the front, the Model 40 allowed passengers to be seated throughout the entire body of the bus. It had two gasoline engines, which were mounted inside the bus on each side. Each engine had its own driveline and differential, and the passenger seats were mounted over the two engine housings.

When the Twin Coach was introduced transit systems in the country's larger cities were looking for a suitable bus model to allow for expansion of their systems and to replace aging streetcars. The Model 40 Twin Coach was exactly the right vehicle at the right time. It met with the approval of city bus operators and many were purchased. In addition to the right fit, the Model 40 proved to be a very dependable vehicle, with some in service for 20 years. The Model 40 was also built for use as a trolley bus.

Smaller cities were also beginning city transit service using buses. Prior to the development of the motorbus,

some small cities had not been able to offer transit service because it was very expensive to begin a streetcar rail system. However, once the appropriate motor vehicles became available, some cities were able to begin operating bus service.

Yellow Coach Manufacturing Co. was another important early city bus builder. Founded in 1923, Yellow Coach was bought by General Motors two years later and renamed Yellow Truck & Coach Manufacturing Co. ACF, which had purchased Fageol Motors, adapted to the changes in the industry and built both city and intercity buses. ACF was one of the first companies to build a bus with the engine underfloor, which helped maximize seating capacity. White Motor Company also produced buses with an underfloor engine. Mack Trucks, like Yellow Coach, eventually featured rear-engine buses.

In the early days, drivers collected fares and would ring up the fares on a register in the upper left corner of the bus. The register rang a big bell every time the driver took money in. Later, registering fare boxes were introduced. They were put in initially to protect the company from drivers taking unauthorized fares.

The Key System provided extensive transit service to Oakland and the East Bay Area of California in 1924. It continued operating for many years, until the public Alameda Contra-Costa Transit Agency was formed. The Key System purchased its first Model 40 Twin Coach in 1927. More were added through 1929, with a total of 45 in the fleet, making it one of the largest fleets of Model 40 buses. The East Bay Motor Coach Lines was the company used by the Key System for bus routes beginning in 1933. *Motor Bus Society*

Brooklyn (New York) Bus Corporation purchased its first four Model 40 Twin Coach buses in 1930, and added two more in 1931. The original Model 40 had two Waukesha engines, but those in Brooklyn had two Hercules engines. Brooklyn also operated one Model 40 Twin Coach trolley bus. The name Brooklyn Bus Corporation was first used in 1929. The Corporation eventually became a subsidiary of Brooklyn & Queens Transit. In 1940 it became a part of the City of New York's transit system. *Motor Bus Society*

Chicago (Illinois) Surface Lines put trolley buses in operation on several routes in the city in 1930. Twin Coach Model 40 TC trolley buses were among the original trolley buses in Chicago. Forty-three of these Twin Coach trolley buses were purchased in 1930, and 15 more were added in 1931. One of these is pictured. The only other cities having more than one of this model Twin Coach trolley bus were Salt Lake City, Utah, Detroit, Michigan, and Duluth, Minnesota. *George Krambles Archive*

In 1930 a tunnel under the Detroit River was built by the Detroit & Canada Tunnel Corporation. The company began operating its own bus service through the one-mile tunnel connecting Detroit, Michigan, and Windsor, Ontario. It purchased 30 Model 40 Twin Coach buses for use in the tunnel. The tunnel service was interesting in several ways. It was one of the first international transit services between the United States and Canada. It operated buses with two-minute headways on the 1.35-mile route, which was two thirds on the company's own property. The Model 40 Twin Coaches were in service through World War II. The City of Detroit now operates the tunnel bus service.

United Electric Railways (UER) of Providence, Rhode Island, began providing transit service in the Providence area in 1921. In July 1922 the first buses went into service. In 1931, approximately when this picture was taken, the UER bus fleet was made up of four makes. Pictured on the left is a Model 40 Twin Coach, one of 69 in the fleet, and the first of 28 that was acquired in 1928. Pictured next is a Model H-7 ACF. There were 14 of these units. The third bus is a Model 54A White with a Brown body, the first of 13 for Providence. The fourth bus is a Yellow Coach Model Z acquired in the mid-1920s. The Rhode Island Public Transit Authority was formed in 1964 to operate all transit service in the state.

The Gillig Corporation of Hayward, California, has a long history in the bus transportation business. Joseph Gillig, a carriage builder, first established his business in 1890. His sons, Leo and Chester, joined the company and named it Gillig Bros. The first buses were built in the 1920s. Pictured here is a 1928 Gillig built on a Fageol chassis. The demand for school buses was increasing, and in 1932 the first Gillig school bus was built. Although intercity, sightseeing, and transit buses were also built, school buses were the company's main product for many years. Gillig changed its emphasis to transit bus production beginning in the 1970s.

The Six Wheel Company of Philadelphia, Pennsylvania, built chassis for buses for four years, between 1924 and 1928. Some 300 buses were built. Four of these buses, with American Motor Body Company bodies built in Detroit, were delivered to Montreal (Quebec) Tramway Company in 1925.

United Railways of St. Louis, Missouri, purchased five Six Wheel Company 27-passenger buses in 1925. They were bodied locally by the St. Louis Car Company. The Six Wheel buses were advertised at the time as being safe and sturdy buses. All Six Wheel Company buses had Continental six-cylinder engines.

Kansas City Railways of Kansas City, Missouri, received 18 of these 63-passenger, open-top double-deck Six Wheel Company buses in 1925. They had St. Louis Car Company bodies. Another five 30-passenger Six Wheel Company buses, with parlor car-style bodies from St. Louis Car Company, were delivered to Kansas City Railways at the same time. All of the Six Wheel Company buses went out of service in Kansas City in 1932. Kansas City Railways was formed in 1916 as a result of a receivership of the Metropolitan Street Railway Co. in 1926. Kansas City Public Service Company became the operator of city service buses in Kansas City.

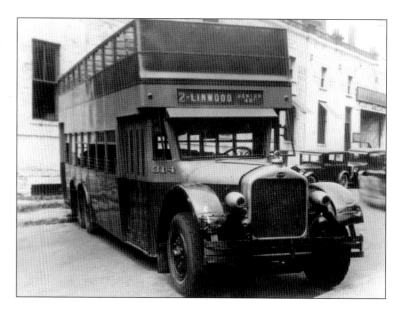

The Versare Corporation of Watervliet, New York, built this unusual six-wheel bus. It was an M 6 HC SCT 37 and was one of five delivered to Montreal, Quebec, in 1928. It accommodated 37 passengers and had a Hercules engine mounted in the rear with an electric drive with two Westinghouse electric motors.

The Versare Corporation was established in Watervliet, New York, in 1925, to produce buses for city service. Its first model was an eight-wheel bus with four wheels in the front and four in the back, mounted on bogies. The front bogie turned as a unit. The Alton Transportation Company, a subsidiary of the Chicago & Alton Railroad, purchased the first two of these buses in 1926. Although these buses were for city service the Alton

Transportation Company operated them on a short intercity line. The buses featured Buda engines and electric drives.

Mack Trucks, Inc. is said to have been the first bus builder in the United States. Early Mack buses were primarily sightseeing models. In the early part of the century Mack chassis were used for city buses. Later, Mack built complete city buses, beginning with the BK chassis. This BK Mack bus went into service in St. Louis, Missouri, in 1930.

United Railways & Electric Company was the pioneer transportation system in Baltimore, Maryland. This Yellow Coach double-deck bus and 11 others entered service in Baltimore in 1930. They were gas-electric buses with seating for 69 passengers. At 14 feet, 3 inches these double-deck buses were very tall.

The Versare Company, famed for building buses with six wheels, also built six-wheel trolley buses. The first 10 of these trolley buses went into service in 1928 for the Utah Light and Traction Company in Salt Lake City. Later the six-wheel trolley buses were converted to two-axle vehicles. In 1928, the Cincinnati Car Corporation acquired the Versare Company and for a time used the Versare name. The Salt Lake City trolley bus pictured, one of seven, was built by the Cincinnati Car Company.

This Reo bus entered service for the Ottawa (Ontario) Electric Railway Company in 1927. It had a 21-passenger body built by the Ottawa Car Body Company. The body was rebuilt in 1931. Ottawa Electric Railway Company was also a Gray Line Sight-seeing company franchisee, and this bus was used for sightseeing.

Chapter 3

Buses Begin Replacing Streetcars

Prior to 1930, the streetcar dominated city transit in the United States and Canada, even in the smaller cities. Bus transportation was unimportant in city service, even though some cities, such as Detroit, Pittsburgh, Los Angeles, and St. Louis, had a few established bus routes prior to 1920. In Canada, the first buses were in service in Winnipeg in 1918 and in Montreal in 1919, according to accounts.

After the early success of buses in New York City and Chicago the number of buses in city service began to grow. Although buses still played a secondary role to the streetcar, they were being recognized for their increasing importance to city transit.

City transit was greatly affected by the Great Depression of the 1930s. The high unemployment rate meant fewer passengers for city systems because people weren't taking the streetcars to their jobs. Meanwhile, the popularity of the mass-produced automobile and the availability of cheap gasoline allowed people to begin commuting with their cars rather than taking the streetcars. This marked the beginning of the dominance of the automobile and the decline in the use of public transportation.

A 30-passenger Mack Model CL bus was first presented in 1932. It had a front engine mounted inside the bus and featured seating for 30 passengers. There were 441 of these small Mack buses produced in five years. A 468-cubic-inch, six-cylinder Mack engine powered the bus. The Rochester (New York) Railways Co-ordinated Bus Lines operated this Model CL. The New York State Railways controlled the company. *Mack Museum*

The B.C. Electric Company operated urban transit in Vancouver, British Columbia, beginning in the early 1900s. It had a large fleet of streetcars, but buses began making an appearance in the 1920s. This bus with a British built chassis was added to the fleet in August 1935. It had a British Leyland chassis with a Hayes Anderson body built in Vancouver. The Hayes Manufacturing Co., Ltd. began in 1928 and built bus bodies for many companies in British Columbia prior to World War II.

In many areas, electric power companies operated the streetcars. Streetcar systems were expensive, both for the initial investment and the ongoing maintenance required. At the time, many operators of streetcar systems were facing aging vehicles and an aging infrastructure, both of which needed replacement. In addition, operators in many northern cities were obligated to clean streets of snow as part of their franchise, another costly part of the operation. These factors combined to cause some power companies not to renew their transportation franchises. Some of these operators abandoned some of their streetcar routes and began using buses, which were flexible, low-cost alternatives. Buses were also used on new routes into the growing suburban areas.

During the 1930s more than 500 cities discontinued streetcar service and substituted buses or trolley cars. In 1935 alone, 34 cities discontinued streetcars and went to all-bus systems. Some streetcar operators discontinued all streetcar service and began operating trolley buses. Because trolley buses operated on electricity, the power companies had the opportunity to continue to supply electric power to transportation vehicles. Trolley bus operations were tried in many locations as early as 1913 and into the 1920s, but most did not last.

Streetcars were not eliminated as quickly in Canada as they were in the United States. Unlike in the United States, many systems in Canada had been municipally owned for some time, and as such were able to survive lean times. Canadians had more loyalty to public transit services, and ridership in most Canadian cities was quite high. In addition, automobile competition was limited, partly because automobiles were not yet equipped to handle the difficult Canadian winters.

A unique private bus service began in 1930 with the opening of a tunnel under the Detroit River, connecting Detroit, Michigan, and Windsor, Ontario. The tunnel was almost a mile long, and provided an appropriate opportunity to operate buses. The Detroit & Canada Tunnel Company operated the 1.35-mile route, which was all on property owned by the tunnel company, with the exception of a few blocks in Detroit.

The 1930s saw a number of significant changes in bus construction. One of these was monocoque construction, a chassis-less design with the body framework supporting the entire bus. It was a welded tubular design, a style sometimes referred to as airplane-type construction.

By the end of the 1930s the diesel engine became the primary engine in most Yellow Coach city and

The British AEC Ranger was one of several buses built in England and used in Vancouver, British Columbia, in the mid-1930s. The bus pictured had a Hayes Anderson body and is shown operating on the busy Grandview Highway route in Vancouver. The bus had two doors and accommodated 25 seated passengers. It was diesel powered. On the radiator was an emblem that read "Oil Engine."

intercity buses. Cummins Engine Company re-powered two buses to run on diesel fuel in 1932. These intercity buses were thought to be the first diesel-powered buses in the United States. The first city bus with a diesel engine was a Twin Coach E Model 37-R DE, which began operating for the Eastern Massachusetts Street Railway in July of 1935. General Motors introduced its first diesel engine in the latter part of the 1930s.

The early diesel engines were four-cycle engines; a large, heavy, and less efficient system than the two-cycle diesel that was developed by General Motors. The two-cycle engine was more reliable, more powerful, and gave a smoother ride, but was not as economical as the four-cycle engine. However, this was not considered a big disadvantage as long as diesel fuel was economical. The two-cycle diesel was used exclusively in Yellow Coach city and intercity buses during the 1930s and 1940s and became the preferred engine in the United States.

General Motors almost completely monopolized two-cycle diesel engine production.

Another innovation was the transversal engine, introduced by Yellow Coach and also by Mack Trucks. The design increased passenger capacity. Underfloor engines were also used in some buses, particularly ACF and White models.

Air brakes were found on city buses as early as 1920. Some early Yellow Coach city buses and a number of buses built by Twin Coach used electric drives to eliminate shifting. Even though many were used in transit buses, these early electric drives proved to be costly and inefficient.

Another early innovation was the semiautomatic transmission known as the Banker. Developed by Yellow Coach/General Motors, it required releasing the accelerator to permit up-shifting. There were continued attempts by several manufacturers to create automatic shifting, and air-shifting systems were available on some buses.

The Detroit (Michigan) Street Railway Company was one of the first municipally operated transportation systems. It continued from its beginning in 1922 through the entire 20th Century and beyond. Buses were introduced early, and in the 1930s there was a trend to operate small buses. The natural choice was to look to Ford for such buses. The first Ford buses, using a Ford chassis and a Union City Body Co. body, went into service in 1934. This Model 51 was introduced at that time, and almost 300 were in service in Detroit. These small buses had 221-cubic-inch, 80-horsepower Ford V-8 engines.

Grand Forks, North Dakota, had a population of 5,500 in 1904. Its first transportation system consisted of one streetcar. It was operated by the Grand Forks Street Railway Co., which was incorporated in 1908. The first two Reo buses to operate in Grand Forks were ordered from Eckland Brothers, Inc., in Minneapolis, Minnesota, in 1930. The last streetcar was operated in Grand Forks in 1934, after which time buses took over the entire service. At that time this White, with an Eckland Brothers body, entered the service, which was then named Grand Forks Transportation Company.

The Ottawa (Ontario) Electric Railway Company acquired this AEC Ranger bus chassis from AEC in England in 1934. The transit body was added by Ottawa Car Body Company. This bus seated 29 passengers. A diesel engine was added in 1937. The original price of the bus was $10,502. At the time, the Ottawa Electric Railway Company operated only 22 buses.

In 1932 Sherbrooke (Quebec) City Transit, Ltd. added four Leyland buses built in England to its fleet. Two were Leyland Lioness buses. The one pictured here was a 21-passenger vehicle. Sherbrooke City Transport Co., Ltd. was a part of Provincial Transport of Montreal, a large intercity bus company. It operated the service from 1932 to 1952. For the next 10 years Services Laramee was the operator. Sherbrooke Transit, Ltd. followed, from 1962 to 1972, when the municipality owned the system.

Kingston (Ontario) City Coach Company began in 1930. It operated the city transit system in the Kingston area until July 1962, when the Kingston Public Utilities acquired the service. Kingston City Coach was originally a subsidiary of Colonial Coach Co. and later a part of Provincial Transport Company. In 1930 two Leyland Lioness buses were acquired. Leyland Motors built Lioness buses in England. A half-cab arrangement and right-hand drive were interesting features of these two buses.

This little bus seating 13 passengers was converted from a Yellow Cab taxi in the Public Service of New Jersey shops in Newark in 1928. It was in service for several years and was the only one of its kind.

The Yellow Coach Model U bus was first introduced in 1930. It was similar to the Yellow Coach Model W. Both of these models were built in city and intercity versions. Wichita (Kansas) Transportation Company purchased five Model U Yellow Coach buses in 1930. One is pictured here as it emerged from the garage. This bus, which had seats for 25 passengers, had a Cadillac V-8 engine.

Oshkosh (Wisconsin) City Lines had been an all-bus property of Wisconsin Power & Light Company when the Fitzgerald brothers purchased it in 1933. The Fitzgeralds bought eight new 18-passenger Yellow Coach Model 709 buses for service in Oshkosh. These small buses had GM 253-cubic-inch, valve-in-head, 76-horsepower engines. Oshkosh City Lines was sold to a local group in 1934. In 1936, the Fitzgerald brothers formed National City Lines, which grew to 26 locations and 862 buses by 1940.

Public Service of New Jersey came up with a plan in 1933 to introduce All Service Vehicles (ASVs). The first ASV was tested using a 1926 Yellow Coach Z-AL-265 gas-electric bus. The first non-converted ASVs went into service in New Jersey in 1935. Between 1935 and 1936, 356 new Yellow Coach ASVs were delivered. Public Service also converted 226 Yellow Coach Model Z buses to operate as ASVs. These interesting vehicles ended their service in 1948.

Eckland Brothers, Inc., of Minneapolis, Minnesota, built the Eckland Dual-Coach in 1933. It had two six-cylinder Waukesha engines, one connected to the back wheels and the other to the front. The Dual-Coach was designed as a city transit bus. It was powerful and very well balanced, but it was heavy and expensive. None were sold and only the prototype was built.

Motor Transit Company of Jacksonville, Florida, operated this 15-passenger Twin Coach bus, which was delivered in 1933. It was the smallest bus built by Twin Coach; just 50 were built. It had a 73-horsepower JXC Hercules engine. In 1929, the operating company in Jacksonville at the time, the Jacksonville Traction Company, acquired four Model 40 Twin Coach buses. Soon after, Jacksonville became an all-bus city. *Motor Bus Society*

In the early 1930s there was a demand for small buses, and the Twin Coach Co. answered the demand with several small models. In 1933 the front-engined Model 23S was introduced. The Duluth-Superior Bus Company of Duluth, Minnesota, acquired 15 of these buses between 1934 and 1936. They operated on an interstate route connecting Duluth with Superior, Wisconsin. Twin Coach buses were very popular in Duluth and Superior for many years.

Louisville (Kentucky) Railway Co. had a history dating back to 1890. In 1923 it established a subsidiary, Kentucky Carriers, Inc., to operate buses, but in 1928 buses operating in Louisville came under Louisville Railway Co. One of the first buses was this 1928 White Model 50B with a Bender body. In 1964 Louisville Railway became known as Louisville Transit Co. At that time it was an all-bus operation. Transit in Louisville came under a public authority in 1974. *American Truck Historical Society*

White Motor Company of Cleveland, Ohio, produced the Model 685 bus between 1932 and 1935. A total of 68 Model 685 buses were built. Trenton (New Jersey) Transit operated one of this type of bus, using it mainly for charter service. A huge 12-cylinder, 811-cubic-inch underfloor gasoline engine powered it. Urban transit began in Trenton in the late 1880s. Trenton Transit Company began in 1929, and became an all-bus system in 1931.

White Motor Company of Cleveland, Ohio, introduced this Model 684 transit bus in 1934. The Virginia Electric & Power Co. in Richmond received the first two of this 32-passenger model. These original White buses had 146-horsepower underfloor engines. At the time, Virginia Electric & Power Co. operated 110 buses in Richmond, 81 in Norfolk, 14 in Petersburg, and 42 in Portsmouth. *American Truck Historical Society*

Indiana Truck Corporation had its beginnings in Marion, Indiana, in 1921. The Brockway Motor Truck Company acquired the company in 1927, and in 1932 the White Motor Company of Cleveland, Ohio, became the new owner. The Indiana name continued. A number of Indiana buses were built, including this Model 16 of 1933. It had a Hercules front-mounted gasoline engine. The Calvetti Transportation Company of Hurley, Wisconsin, owned this Model 16 Indiana bus. It ran on an hourly schedule between Hurley and Ironwood, Michigan. The small company also had an intercity route to Mellen, Wisconsin. *American Truck Historical Society*

The Illinois Power and Light Corporation of Peoria, Illinois, was one of the many electric companies that first operated streetcars in large and small cities and later turned to buses. This company operated city services in Danville, Galesburg, Quincy, and Peoria, Illinois, and other cities. The company disposed of the transit systems in the mid-1930s. This 1935 White Model 706M bus, and three others like it, operated in Danville. Soon after, the Danville system became Danville City Lines, one of the early National City Lines properties.

Chicago (Illinois) Surface Lines began using buses in 1927 and operated Twin Coach and ACF models. In 1935 the company turned to White Motor Company for buses and had almost 600 in its fleet, the last units being large Model 798 Whites in 1948. Pictured here is one of 33 two-door Model 805-M White buses. This bus had a similar body to the one-door Model 706-M White. Chicago Surface Lines, incorporated in 1927, was a large operator of streetcars. Twenty years later the Chicago Transit Authority was established and took over the Chicago Surface Lines.

This Mack Model CY bus was one of five in the fleet of Fort William (Ontario) Utilities. It was acquired in 1941. The Model CY Mack was first introduced in early 1938 and was the first to be built by Mack with unitized construction. When manufacturing ended in 1941, 329 had been built. Many Model CY Mack buses were sold in Canada. The cities of Fort William and neighboring Port Arthur joined in 1970 to become Thunder Bay, and the transit system became united as Thunder Bay Transit. Electric streetcars began in the area in 1891, and ended after World War II, when trolley buses were introduced.

The Miami (Florida) Transit Company operated this Mack Model L3G in 1940. Mack began building the L Series buses in 1939 and continued building them until 1941. Miami Transit Company had its start in 1940, and acquired the City of Miami transit operations. Streetcars were discontinued at that time. Miami had 208 buses, many of which were Macks. Miami Transit ended operations in 1962 when the Miami-Dade Transit Agency was formed.

Twin City Motor Bus Company was incorporated in 1915 and was acquired by the Twin City Rapid Transit Co. in 1921. The two companies operated transit services in the Minneapolis and St. Paul, Minnesota, areas. One of the routes operated by the Twin City Motor Bus Company was an express service along University Avenue between Minneapolis and St. Paul. In 1934, 12 Model 716 Yellow Coach buses, one of which is pictured here, were acquired. Three more were purchased in 1935.

The first trolley buses built by Yellow Truck & Coach were introduced in 1932. The first model was known as a Type 44, Model 701. The Wisconsin Gas and Electric Company of Kenosha, Wisconsin, purchased 12 of these first-and-only Model 701 Yellow Coach trolley buses. The Kenosha trolley bus operation, which continued for 20 years, was one of the smallest trolley bus operations in the United States. Kenosha also had the distinction of having a transit system with no other vehicles except trolley buses. Yellow Coach built 456 other trolley buses, including 346 All Service Vehicles (ASVs) for Public Service of New Jersey.

Indianapolis (Indiana) Railways, Inc. was established in 1932, although transit in the Indiana capital city had its beginnings as early as the mid-19th Century. Motorbus service began in the early 1920s. Trolley bus service had its start in Indianapolis in 1934, when 15 Brill T-40 trolley buses went into service. Pictured here is one of the 57 Brill T-40S trolley buses delivered in 1937. Indianapolis had 152 trolley buses in service prior to World War II. *Motor Bus Society*

Although urban transportation began in Columbus, Ohio, much earlier, the Columbus Railway, Power & Light Co. became the operator of streetcars in the city in 1914. It began its first motorbus line in 1926, and then inaugurated trolley bus service in 1933. Pictured is one of the 40 Brill/General Electric trolley buses acquired in 1938. The Brill company was a leading trolley bus builder in the United States at the time. Brill, with ACF-Brill Motors, built nearly 2,000 trolley buses between 1921 and 1952. Columbus ended trolley bus service in 1965. *Motor Bus Society*

Duluth-Superior Transit Company of Duluth, Minnesota, began running trolley buses in 1931. The company had the first Brill Model 40 SMT trolley buses built. Ten of these trolley buses were added in 1939, and by 1944 there were 32 units in the fleet consisting of Brill, Twin Coach and Pullman Standard vehicles. Brill built 266 of the Model 40 SMT trolley buses between 1936 and 1942. Trolley bus service in Duluth ended in 1957. No trolley buses operated in Superior, Wisconsin.

Portland, Oregon, was one of many cities throughout the country that began trolley bus service in the mid-1930s. The Portland Traction Company operated the system. The first trolley buses entered service in Portland in 1936. At that time 60 Mack Model CR 35 units were purchased. Another 60, one of which is pictured here, were added soon afterward. Portland was the best customer Mack had for its trolley buses. There were 141 in the fleet. In 1958 trolley bus service ended in Portland.

Beaver Metropolitan Coaches, Inc. of Beaver Falls, Pennsylvania, began building buses in the mid-1930s. Its first buses were on Ford chassis with Ford engines mounted inside in the front. Capital Transit Co. in Washington, D.C., purchased 15 of these Model 500 Beaver buses in 1938. They joined a very mixed fleet in Washington. Capital Transit originated in 1933, following numerous companies that operated transit in the nation's capital. Capital Transit was followed by DC Transit in 1956.

St. Louis (Missouri) Public Service Company purchased 10 Model 731 Yellow Coach buses in 1935. The one pictured here was the first Model 731 built. The St. Louis Public Service Co. acquired a total of 100 of these buses through 1938. They carried the name Peoples Motor Bus Company and generally operated on special routes throughout St. Louis. The Model 731 bus had a transversally mounted gasoline engine in the rear.

Evanston (Illinois) Railway Company, a subsidiary of the Evanston & Niles Center Bus Company, existed for only three years, from 1935 to 1937. It operated some bus service in Evanston. In 1935 the Evanston Railway Company purchased 15 of these Model 728 Yellow Coach buses to replace streetcars. The Model 728 had a 450-cubic-inch GM gasoline engine mounted transversally in the rear. It accommodated 32 passengers. It was especially popular in medium-sized cities, many of which discontinued streetcars in the 1930s. Yellow Coach built 1,156 units of this bus model between 1935 and 1939.

Chapter 4

Nickel Fares Prevail

By 1930 trolley bus technology had improved. Trolley bus numbers were growing in the United States and trolley buses were beginning to replace streetcars. In 1941 there were approximately 3,000 trolley buses in service. (This included about 355 All Service Vehicle Yellow Coach trolley buses for Public Service of New Jersey. ASVs operated mainly as electric trolley buses, but also had an auxiliary gasoline engine.) Not only did trolley buses give the power companies an opportunity to sell their electricity, in addition trolley buses were superior to the early diesel buses in climbing hills. They were needed in cities with many steep hills, such as San Francisco and Seattle.

More cities were discontinuing streetcar service in favor of buses. Houston, Texas, became the largest all-bus city in 1940. The following year both Honolulu and Seattle scrapped their streetcars, but each retained trolley buses. Seattle also had a large fleet of gasoline buses.

The Public Utilities Holding Act of 1935 ruled that companies that operated electric power systems had to divest themselves of their transit systems and any other

Bee Line Transit Corporation of Westville, Illinois, began bus service in suburban Danville, Illinois, in 1936. This 26-passenger bus was the fifth one in the fleet. It was built on a Chevrolet chassis with a 216 engine. Wayne Works of Richmond, Indiana, built the body. The Bee Line was the beginning of the American Transit Corporation, which was headed by the Giacoma brothers, Dominic and Peter, and Henry DeTournay. The American Transit Corporation empire at one time included transit properties in some 30 cities.

Palo Alto (California) Transit served an area of then-small cities on the peninsula south of San Francisco. The cities included Stanford, the home of famed Stanford University. The company eventually became a part of Santa Clara County Transportation Agency in San Jose. This 1935 bus on a Diamond T chassis has a Gillig Bros. body. Although Gillig was a large producer of school buses, it also built a number of transit, sightseeing, and intercity buses. Gillig operated its factory in San Francisco when this bus was built. Gillig Bros. moved to larger quarters in Hayward, California, in 1938.

subsidiary businesses. Consequently, many cities lost their streetcar systems. However, this ruling did not affect companies that did all of their business within one state, and some transit systems, such as those in New Orleans and in St. Joseph, Missouri, remained in private hands.

The system in New Orleans, New Orleans Public Service, Inc. (NOPSI), was particularly interesting. It charged a very low fare, which was subsidized by the sale of electricity by the power system. Even as costs went up, New Orleans continued to subsidize buses.

In the period immediately preceding World War II there was continuing activity in the city-bus business. The operation of city transit systems was changed when E. Roy Fitzgerald and his four brothers established Rex Finance Company in Chicago. They began acquiring various transit systems, often taking over systems that

had been abandoned by electric power companies. The Fitzgeralds stepped in and established new service, usually with new buses.

National City Lines, the company formed by the Fitzgeralds, would become an empire in the transit bus business. In the beginning, National City Lines had its ups and downs, largely due to a lack of financing during the difficult Depression years. However, by 1936, 17 city bus systems in five different states carried the National City Lines name.

National City Lines gained prominence in the bus industry, and in other industries, for the way it conducted business. The company emphasized strict cost controls, quality maintenance, and standardization of buses and products. To improve efficiency, new garages were built in many of the cities where National City Lines operated.

Most of the National City Lines properties charged a five-cent fare, a fare that was widely publicized. The nickel fare was a sign of the times, at a time when a quart of milk was only 10 cents. Most cities promoted the five-cent fare, but offered discounted fares by selling tokens at a discount rate.

In the late 1940s and early 1950s National City Lines bought more small- and medium-sized city transit systems. There were 41 subsidiary companies carrying the National City Lines name in 1954. Some of the companies were operated by Pacific City Lines, which began in 1938. National City Lines had an interest in Pacific City Lines and eventually acquired the company.

National City Lines also began investing in larger bus systems. St. Louis Public Service Company was the first. Then Baltimore Transit, Los Angeles Transit, and the Key System in Oakland, California had National City Lines investment, with National City Lines people involved in the management.

At about the same time another city transit consolidation was taking place. It would become American Transit Corporation. Its principals were the Giacoma brothers, Dominic and Pete, and Henry DeTournay and A. J. de Mayo. Several other companies were operated similarly, with transit properties in several cities. It appears that consolidations were quite common in the city bus business as early as the 1930s and 1940s.

In the 1930s, city transit operators were demanding smaller buses. The Twin Coach Co. responded to the demand with several new models, including the Model 23R, which is believed to be the first low-floor bus. The company also built an articulated bus, but it was ahead of its time and only two were eventually built.

In 1936 Yellow Coach built new-style double-deck city buses for New York City's Fifth Avenue Coach Company and the Chicago Motor Coach Company, which revived the old double-deck idea for city buses. These marked the last of the double deckers for city service in the United States. Only New York City and Chicago operated them.

Ford Motor Company, which had been building chassis for buses for a number of years, introduced a rear-engine, 27-passenger transit bus in 1939. It became very popular, with several thousand operating throughout the country in cities large and small. Detroit was said to have had 1,000 of these buses in service at one point in time.

In 1936 Paul O. Dittmar, owner of the South Suburban Safeway Lines of Harvey, Illinois, ventured into the bus-building business under the name Dittmar Manufacturing Company. A small 25- to 35-passenger bus, called the DMX, was the result. The DMX was built for both city and intercity service. Most were city buses. In fact, South Suburban Safeway Lines operated 33 of the 150 units built. Either Ford V-8 or Hercules engines were used. Waterloo, Cedar Falls, and Northern Railroad operated the DMX buses pictured here. These cities operated interurban rail services, as well as city service in the Waterloo area. Details about the buses are unknown.

The Pittsburgh, Pennsylvania, area has many small communities surrounding the city. These communites are rich in history, and many had separate transit systems as well as services operating into Pittsburgh. Beaver Falls is one of these communities. It had its own street railway system as early as 1885. As streetcars lost their importance in small cities, bus companies not only replaced the streetcars, but also built up sizable bus operating systems. Beaver Valley Motor Coach Company was one company that served the Beaver Valley for 55 years. The company began building its own buses in 1934. The next year, bus building for other companies began under the name Beaver Metropolitan Coaches, Inc. Beaver continued in business until 1956. One of the first buses built by Beaver Metropolitan Coaches was this 22-passenger Model 101 in 1935.

The Flxible Company of Loudonville, Ohio, began bus building in 1924. Flxible's primary product was the intercity bus. However, one small city bus, known as the Model 21 CT, was built in 1935. The Model 21 CT featured a Chevrolet chassis and a 6-cylinder, 60-horsepower Chevrolet engine. The Flxible Co. remained an important intercity bus builder until 1952, when it worked out an agreement with the Twin Coach Co. to produce city buses. Intercity bus production ended in 1970, and the Flxible Co. became an exclusive builder of transit buses.

Fargo Motors Corporation, a division of the Chrysler Corporation, introduced buses in 1930. Fargo became the name of the buses formerly built by Dodge Brothers and Graham Brothers, both connected with Chrysler. Fargo built only four models. The Model 90 was designed for city service. The 37 Fargo Model 90 and Model 94 buses operated by the Spokane (Washington) United Railways was the largest number in any transit fleet. Most of these were Model 90s. They had 284.8-cubic-inch, eight-cylinder engines. Production of Fargo buses ended in 1933. Spokane United Railways began in 1922 with streetcar services. In 1936 all streetcars were retired.

Johnstown (Pennsylvania) Traction Company operated 14 Yellow Coach Model 733 buses. The one pictured here was built in 1937. The Model 733 was first introduced in 1936, and had the distinction of being the greatest number of any one bus built by Yellow Coach with 1,462 units produced. Johnstown had horse-drawn trams as early as 1883. Johnstown Traction Company came into existence in 1910, and in 1922, Traction Bus Company, a part of Johnstown Traction Co., opened its doors. Johnstown had streetcars and trolley buses in service, as well as several bus routes.

Wisconsin Power & Light Company, headquartered in Madison, operated city bus systems in Beloit, Fond du Lac, Janesville, and Sheboygan, Wisconsin. The company also operated an intercity bus route, called the Orange Line, between Green Bay and Madison. For the city services Wisconsin Power & Light Company operated Yellow Coach Model 1204 (later TG 24) buses. These were small 24-passenger buses that were first introduced in 1938. A Chevrolet 216-cubic-inch engine was mounted transversally in the rear.

Bus 899 was a special bus built on a Ford chassis in 1936. It had full wheel coverings, two doors, and a 221-cubic-inch Ford V-8 engine. The Detroit (Michigan) Street Railway operated it in regular service until 1943. Ford built no other buses of this type.

In 1937 the Ford Motor Co. of Dearborn, Michigan, in conjunction with the body builder Union City Body Company, came out with the Model 70, 27-passenger bus. It had a front-mounted, 95-horsepower Ford V-8 engine. Pictured is the first one built, which was delivered to the City of Detroit-Department of Street Railways. It was one of 750 of this type bus, which was in service in Detroit for 10 years.

Wisconsin Michigan Power Company of Appleton, Wisconsin, purchased these two Ford Model 70 buses in 1937. The Model 70 had Union City bodies, Ford forward-control chassis, and 85-horsepower Ford V-8 engines. Wisconsin Michigan Power Company began operating buses in Appleton and adjoining cities in 1927. It was succeeded by the Appleton Motor Coach Lines, which served the area until 1955. Fox River Bus Lines then operated the service. Valley Transit, the present publicly operated company, came into existence in the Appleton area in 1978.

In 1941 the Toronto (Ontario) Transportation Commission acquired 22 Model 19-B Ford Transit Buses. They were the only ones in the Toronto fleet and operated primarily during World War II. Most Ford Transit Buses that operated in Canada had chassis built by Ford in Windsor, Ontario, and bodies built by Brantford (Ontario) Coach and Body Company.

The rear-engined Ford Transit Bus was introduced in 1939. It became a very popular bus and was seen in both large and small cities in the United States and Canada. Some were exported, and the advertising slogan, "The sun never sets on a Ford Transit Bus," was probably true. Kitchener (Ontario) Public Utilities Commission was one of the many Canadian companies that operated Ford Transit Buses. This one was pictured in its final years with rounded windshield corners to better secure the windshield. Kitchener operated a number of these Ford Transit Buses, the first of which they ordered in 1940. The first buses operated in Kitchener in 1939. The city was originally named Berlin, but the name was changed during World War I. Transit had been operating in Berlin as early as 1883. In 1973, the name of the system was changed to Kitchener Transit.

The FitzJohn Coach Company of Muskegon, Michigan, built primarily intercity model buses for a number of years, although some city buses were built with chassis by Reo, Chevrolet, and others. In 1940, the Model 300 was presented. Pictured here is one of the Model 300 FitzJohn buses which was acquired by Carier et Frere of Shawinigan Falls, Quebec, a company which operated city service in Shawinigan Falls and Trois Riviers, Quebec, for many years. Carier et Frere also had intercity routes to Montreal and Quebec City, and was a good FitzJohn customer for both city and intercity buses. *Motor Bus Society*

The Dayton-Xenia Railway Company of Dayton, Ohio, was best known for its streetcars and trolley buses. Dayton-Xenia began in 1906, and in 1940 began operating trolley buses. In 1955 it merged with the City Railway Company in Dayton. The Dayton & Xenia Motor Bus Company was formed in 1937 and operated buses in the area, including this Model 782 White, which had a 362-cubic-inch underfloor engine. This model White was built for just three years, from 1940 to 1942, although some additional units were built in 1946.

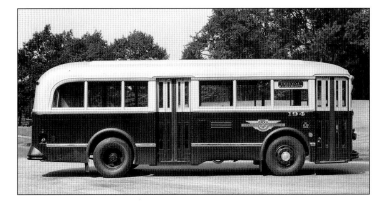

The Washington, Virginia & Maryland Coach Co. (WV&M) was formed in 1926. It was sometimes known as the Arnold Lines after its founder, Leon Arnold. It operated routes from suburban areas of Arlington, Virginia, to Washington, D.C. The company also had a route into Maryland near the Potomac. In 1940, 15 Model 782 White buses were added to a mixed WV&M fleet. The White 782 was a 32-passenger model. It had a 362-cubic-inch, six-cylinder underfloor gasoline engine.

Reo Motors Inc. began building rear-engined chassis for buses in 1937 with the Model 3P7. The Reo pictured here had a FitzJohn Model 350 body. It was one of 10 delivered to City Transport in Lansing, Michigan, Reo's hometown. Lansing had bus service as early as 1922. In 1933, when streetcar service ended, City Transport Corporation came into being. For a time afterward National City Lines operated the Lansing transit system. Reo continued to build buses for Lansing until 1953. Soon afterward, Reo bus production ended.

Oklahoma Railway Company, which operated city bus service in Oklahoma City, purchased 10 of the first Model LC buses from Mack Trucks in 1940, and 10 more the following year. The Model LC Mack had a six-cylinder EN-457 gasoline engine mounted in the rear. There were more than 500 of the LC Macks built. Transportation in Oklahoma City began in 1902, when Oklahoma was still a territory. In 1904 the Oklahoma City Railway was formed. The Oklahoma Railway Company was the name later used. It was purchased in 1945, along with Oklahoma Transportation Company, an intercity bus company.

The Los Angeles (California) Railway operated urban service in the Los Angeles metropolitan area between 1895 and 1945, although with slight name changes during the period. Eighteen of these small Yellow Coach Model TD 3205 buses were added in 1941. Four more were purchased the next year. Production of this model began in 1941 and continued for two years. A total of 265 units, both gasoline and diesel, were built. Following World War II, Los Angeles Railway was acquired by new owners and became Los Angeles Transit Lines.

ACF Motors of Philadelphia, Pennsylvania, was a major producer of both city and intercity buses in the pre-World War II period. ACF built 4,322 buses between 1933 and 1943. One of the models was the H-13-S. In late 1938, Fort Worth (Texas) Transit purchased five ACF Model H-13-S buses, one of which is pictured here. These buses used Hall-Scott 166 engines mounted under the floor. Fort Worth had transit in 1874 and electric companies operated the services for a long period, up until 1937, when Fort Worth Transit Co. began. A public authority replaced Fort Worth Transit Co. in 1972.

This Model H-17-S ACF bus was one of 15 ordered by the Dallas (Texas) Railway & Terminal Company in 1937. The Model H-17-S was the most popular city bus built by ACF Motors in Philadelphia prior to World War II. There were a total of 551 built between 1935 and 1938. The Dallas Railway & Terminal Company had only 79 buses at the time, but operated 215 streetcars over 117 miles of track in Dallas. *Motor Bus Society*

The Philadelphia and West Chester (Pennsylvania) Traction Company operated suburban trains in the Philadelphia area for many years. In 1922, a bus subsidiary called Aronimink Transportation Company began. Some of the company's early buses were Fageols, Twin Coaches, and Macks. In the mid-1930s, when the bus subsidiary had 85 buses, ACF Model H-17-S buses were operated, one of which is pictured here. The name Red Arrow Lines had been adopted for the rail and bus operations. In 1970, the Southeastern Pennsylvania Transportation Authority acquired Red Arrow Lines. *Motor Bus Society*

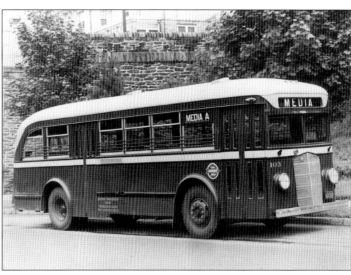

The Twin Coach Model 37 RDE was the first city bus in the United States with a diesel engine, a Hercules DKXB. It was mounted transversally in the rear and had an electric drive. Eastern Massachusetts Street Railway of Boston, Massachusetts, purchased this bus in July 1935, and it remained in service for a number of years. Eastern Massachusetts Street Railway Company operated an extensive network of urban and interurban transit services in Eastern Massachusetts. Local service was provided in Quincy, Lowell, Lynn, Taunton, Attleboro, and other cities. Most of the cities discontinued streetcar service in the mid-1930s, except for Quincy, which had streetcars until 1948. The Massachusetts Bay Transportation Authority acquired the company in 1968.

Six Model 30 GS Twin Coach buses joined the Duluth-Superior Transit Company of Duluth, Minnesota, in 1942. Twin Coach began building this style bus in 1935. Known as the Model 23 R, these buses had Hercules engines mounted above the rear axles, resulting in no rear wheel or differential housings. Therefore, the buses had a flat floor and low entry. As buses became larger, this style became impractical because the wheelbase had to be lengthened even further. The Model 30 GS was not produced until 1940, but it was popular, and in four years 577 units were built. Duluth-Superior Transit was a very good Twin Coach customer.

Chapter 5

Important Wartime Role

Bus transportation played an important part in keeping the country moving during World War II. Although new bus manufacturing was curtailed, and manufacturing plants went into production of military vehicles and equipment, the shortage of buses was addressed. A limited number of buses were built and were referred to as "ODTs," after the Office of Defense Transportation, which gave its official authorization. These buses were usually put into service immediately, with no more than a coat of primer applied.

Transit systems limped along during the war years. Older buses had to be returned to service. With spare parts scarce and with the fleets aging, improvisation sometimes became necessary to keep the buses running. The time serves as a tribute to the people operating the

Chicago (Illinois) Motor Coach Company was one of the pioneer city bus systems and also one of the first to serve with double-deck buses. Double-deck buses continued to be on the Chicago scene into the 1930s. In 1933 a new rear-engined double-deck bus seating 73 passengers was tested. Yellow Truck & Coach built the bus. After successful testing, the Model 720, as it was designated, was ordered by the Chicago Motor Coach Company: the first one in 1934 and 100 more in 1936. These buses had a GM 707-cubic-inch gasoline engine mounted transversally in the rear, and a semiautomatic transmission. They ran regular service until 1950.

This was an unusual bus that was operated by the Suburban Transportation System in the Seattle area in 1934. George Yost, who owned Suburban, was responsible for the design of the bus. It was a tractor-trailer arrangement using a Ford V-8 truck for power and a trailer body built by Seattle's Tricoach Corporation. The driver actually sat in the trailer and steered the vehicle from that position. The bus had this unusual design because Suburban Transportation drove its buses onto the ferry dock in Edmonds, Washington, to pick up ferryboat passengers. With this design the buses could turn around on the dock and didn't have to back up, as did other buses in the Suburban fleet.

transit systems. And while it was often more difficult to keep the buses on the road, some cities were finding it necessary to expand routes in order to serve military bases and defense plants. Some cities used trailer buses to accommodate the large number of military and defense workers.

For the first time women drove buses, and were being recruited as drivers in many cities. It was Rosie the Riveter in war plants and Rosie the Bus Driver for transit systems. After the war the women went back to being housewives. It was years before women bus drivers were found in significant numbers again.

Ridership during the war surged throughout the United States and Canada. For example, buses carried just over 13 billion passengers in 1940. In 1944, the figure was more than 23 billion. In Honolulu alone, the ridership soared from 38.5 million passengers in 1940 to 124.8 million in 1944.

In addition to passengers, buses carried advertising and promotions for the war effort. War bond advertisements, armed forces recruitment messages, and other promotions were seen painted on buses and on posters at bus stations and stops. The industry extended an all-out effort that proved vital.

In November 1938 ACF Motors in Philadelphia introduced the Model 26-U bus. Only 50 of this model were built before production ended in 1941. They had Hall-Scott Model 95 gasoline engines mounted under the floor. Staten Island Coach Co. purchased the first 36 units built. This was the largest order for this ACF bus. Staten Island, or the Borough of Richmond, in New York City had horse cars as early as 1867 and even an early trolley bus line in the 1920s. Staten Island Coach Co. began in 1933 and existed only 13 years. After its demise, another company operated the system for a short period, and then the New York City Transit Authority became the new operator.

The Twin Coach Co. was very innovative in producing a variety of buses from the revolutionary Model 40 Twin Coach, first built in 1927. An interesting articulated bus was built in late 1938 and delivered to the Baltimore (Maryland) Transit Company. It was different than the modern articulated buses because it was hinged in the middle for vertical flexibility. It also had four axles, with two stationed at the hinged section. A Hercules DRXB diesel engine with an electric drive was mounted in the rear. Prior to World War II, Baltimore Transit Co. operated other Twin Coaches in its fleet, as well as ACF and Yellow Coach buses. Trolley buses operated in Baltimore from 1922 to 1931 and again from 1938 to 1959.

Baltimore (Maryland) Transit Company was a subsidiary of the United Railways & Electric Company. In 1935 that became the official name for the streetcar, trolley bus, and bus system in Baltimore, although trolley bus operations didn't begin until 1938. Between 1936 and 1938, 42 Twin Coach Model 40 RGE diesel-electric buses were added to the fleet. This Model 40 RGE Twin Coach was one of 18 with diesel power. Twin Coach introduced the first diesel-engined buses in 1935. Hercules Engine Company built the engines. *Motor Bus Society*

Yellow Truck & Coach Division of General Motors of Pontiac, Michigan, introduced a new model bus in 1939. It was the Model TC 4501, which was similar to the Model 740, but was longer and seated 45 passengers. Chicago (Illinois) Motor Coach Company purchased the first 44 units, which were the only units of this model built in 1939. These buses had GM 6-71 diesel engines. When the Chicago Transit Authority purchased Chicago Motor Coach Company in 1952, these buses came into the Transit Authority's fleet, but were retired soon afterward. The Chicago Motor Coach Company possessed a rich history, which began in 1917. The service was referred to as the "Boulevard Route" and operated on Chicago's Lake Shore Boulevard and other important Chicago boulevards and streets.

Seattle (Washington) Transit System began replacing its streetcars in 1940. Trolley buses were chosen as replacement vehicles on most routes. Twin Coach Model 41 GWFT trolley buses were chosen, and 135 units were ordered, one of which is pictured here. This was the largest order for trolley buses in the United States prior to World War II. Trolley buses had the reputation of being able to negotiate steep grades, and Seattle had some routes on hilly streets. Trolley buses continue to operate in Seattle today, some using an all-trolley bus tunnel under the city's downtown area.

Pictured is a one-of-a-kind trolley bus. It was built by Motor Coach Industries of Winnipeg, Manitoba, in 1942, and was known as Model TRY. Winnipeg Electric Company was the owner of this trolley bus. Winnipeg began operating trolley buses in 1938 and continued operating buses until 1970. This Model TRY ran until 1960. Motor Coach Industries was a major producer of intercity buses and was owned by Western Canadian Greyhound Lines, beginning in 1948. In 1958 Greyhound Lines in the United States became the full owner of the company.

Chapter 6

Diesel Power and Trolley Buses

General Motors had a major interest in Yellow Coach, and in 1943 purchased a minority interest. Yellow Coach became a wholly owned division and adopted a new name, GM Truck and Coach Division. Although General Motors did not make major changes in the city buses Yellow Coach had built before the war, sales were excellent in the postwar years. Most were sold with diesel engines.

Because of the lack of new bus production during World War II, fleet replacement became a priority after the war. In 1945, a war plant in Fort William, Ontario, was quickly converted to build buses. The Canadian counterpart of ACF-Brill Motors in Philadelphia began building transit and intercity buses at the Fort Williams plant under the CCF-Brill name. Both CCF-Brill and ACF-Brill produced similar transit, intercity, and trolley buses, making some changes from prewar models.

Marmon-Herrington Inc. of Indianapolis, Indiana, had a rich history building automobiles and military vehicles, first under the Marmon name. The Marmon-Herrington venture began in 1931. After World War II the company began building trolley buses. That undertaking was successful, but trolley buses were largely phased out of the American scene in the late 1950s. The company ended production in 1955, after building some 1,500 units. The Milwaukee (Wisconsin) and Suburban Transport Company bought 52 Model TC 44 Marmon-Herrington trolley buses in 1947 and 1948. Other Marmon-Herrington trolley buses saw service in Milwaukee after being acquired from Indianapolis. Trolley bus service in Milwaukee ended in 1965.

The St. Louis (Missouri) Car Company was primarily a builder of streetcars and passenger railroad cars beginning in 1887. The company also built some double-deck bus bodies as early as 1914, and in the early 1920s built four experimental trolley buses for Windsor, Ontario. Then, in 1930, St. Louis Car Company became a major builder of trolley buses. In 21 years 1,119 trolley buses were built. The San Francisco (California) Municipal Railway (MUNI) operated 16 St. Louis trolley buses prior to World War II. In 1951 MUNI purchased 40 of the last 90 units built. One is pictured here in downtown San Francisco. Trolley bus operations began in San Francisco in 1935, and today there continues to be a large fleet of trolley buses operating transit service in San Francisco.

Other companies producing postwar transit buses included Twin Coach, Mack Trucks, White Motor Company, Reo Motors Inc., Beaver Metropolitan Coaches, and the FitzJohn Body Co. A new bus, the Southern Coach, was also launched in 1946.

At the beginning of the war Ford had been building a number of small buses in conjunction with Union City Body Company, which furnished the bodies. After the war Ford and Union City Body parted company, and Ford began to build its own buses using bodies built by Wayne Works of Richmond, Indiana. Eventually, Marmon-Herrington of Indianapolis took over the Ford program. Union City Body Company joined with a new company, Transit Bus, to produce a new model known as the Transit Bus. These buses had Union City bodies. Eventually Checker Motors took over Transit Bus, but only for a short period of time, after which production of buses was discontinued.

Technology changes were very important in the postwar years. Most buses had the new, and very popular, two-cycle General Motors diesel engine. General Motors enjoyed excellent sales in the postwar period. Its large transit buses were equipped with transverse-mounted rear engines and the new torque converter in the "V" drive configuration.

Twin Coach introduced major changes to its buses after the war, not only in appearance, but also in the engines and suspension. The postwar buses featured a six-piece slanted windshield and large side windows, along with underfloor gasoline engines and Torsilastic suspensions.

After the war the market seemed to be good for larger buses, and the Model 58-D articulated Twin Coach was introduced. In 1948 the Omaha & Council Bluffs (Nebraska) Street Railway Company ordered its first articulated Twin Coach. Nine more were later delivered. Except for one other bus, these were the only model 58-D Twin Coaches sold, and they served in Omaha for a number of years.

Kenworth Motor Truck Company in Seattle, Washington, a well-known manufacturer of trucks for many years, also built a limited number of buses for both city and intercity services. Portland (Oregon) Traction Company acquired 50 Model E Kenworth trolley buses. By the mid-1950s Kenworth discontinued bus building and placed total emphasis on trucks.

Between 1945 and 1949 more than 4,000 trolley buses were built for cities in the United States and Canada. Trolley bus manufacturers included ACF-Brill, CCF-Brill, St. Louis Car Company, the Pullman-Standard Company, and Twin Coach. Marmon-Herrington also entered the trolley bus market.

In the late 1940s National City Lines was named in an antitrust suit involving exclusive supply contracts with companies having investments in National City Lines. It wasn't until 1955 that the company signed a consent decree in which it agreed to purchase supplies on a competitive-bid basis. Meanwhile, the suppliers with investments in the company, which included GM Truck and Coach Division, Mack Trucks, Firestone Tire & Rubber Co., and others, discontinued their investments in National City Lines.

Winnipeg, Manitoba, was the second city in Canada to operate trolley buses. (Montreal was the first.) The Winnipeg Electric Company started trolley bus service in 1938 with 11 Mack vehicles. More Macks were added in 1940 and 1943. In 1945 Winnipeg added 15 Pullman-Standard Model 44 AS trolley buses. Later, 35 more were acquired. After World War II more than 100 CCF-Brill trolley buses were purchased, adding to the Winnipeg fleet. The trolley bus service continued until 1970.

Johnstown (Pennsylvania) Traction Company (JTC) was the last transit system in the United States to begin a trolley bus system. That was in 1951. Six new St. Louis Car Co. trolley buses were acquired. When streetcars were discontinued in Johnstown in 1960, JTC added a number of used trolley buses. Ten 1939 Brill Model 40 SMT units and six 1952 ACF-Brill T 46 trolley buses, one of which is pictured here, came from Cincinnati, Covington, and Newport Street Railway Company (Green Line), which also sent five Marmon-Herrington trolley buses to Johnstown. Trolley bus service ended in Johnstown in 1967.

The New Orleans (Louisiana) Public Service, Inc. (NOPSI) was a good customer for White Model 788 40-passenger buses. The first 13 went into service in 1940, followed by 66 more. After World War II NOPSI added 185 more Model 788 White buses. They all had Hydro-Torque transmissions. One of these Whites is pictured in New Orleans' French Quarter. Although New Orleans had public transportation in the mid-1800s, the New Orleans Public Service was formed later and controlled transit, electricity, and gas in the city for many years. It wasn't until 1983 that a public transit agency was established. New Orleans was the last large city to create a public transit agency.

The Waukegan & North Chicago Transit Company began service in Waukegan, Illinois, and several surrounding communities in 1948. The operation had been transferred from the Chicago, North Shore, and Milwaukee Railroad, an electric line between Chicago and Milwaukee via Waukegan. In 1947, during the railroad's ownership, five White Model 788s were acquired. This White model was introduced in 1937. It was a 40-passenger bus with a 12-cylinder underfloor engine.

DC Transit became the operator of the transit system in Washington, D.C. in 1956. Capital Transit, the previous operator, was forced to close down. It had been involved in a six-week strike and problems with the governing body, which at that time regulated transit in the city. There were 388 streetcars operating on Washington streets. Buses replaced streetcars a year after DC Transit took over. By 1960 there were no longer streetcars in Washington. When DC Transit took over, the new company acquired a number of Capital Transit buses, including this 1947 Model 789 White. A number of Model 788 Whites and newer 1144 and 1150DW model Whites were also transferred to DC Transit. The newer Whites had Hydro-Torque drives. DC Transit lasted until 1972, when the Washington Metropolitan Area Transit Authority (WMATA) was formed.

Colorado Springs, Colorado, had horse cars as early as 1886, and streetcar service soon followed. Buses began in 1931 with the name Colorado Springs Bus Co. Buses built by White Motor Company were favored, and in 1945, 10 Model 788 40-passenger buses were acquired, one of which is pictured here. The same year, 12 Model 798 Whites, seating 44 passengers, were added. This ended the domination of White buses in Colorado Springs. A variety of buses followed, including Fords, Transit Buses, ACF-Brills, and General Motors buses.

The White Motor Company of Cleveland, Ohio, didn't introduce new model transit buses immediately following World War II, but continued to sell its Model 798 transit buses to a number of customers. A postwar model was in the plans. The 1100 Series was announced in 1946, but actual production did not begin until 1949. Mainly it had a restyled front. The large Model 1144 had a 12-cylinder underfloor gasoline engine. A diesel engine was also available. Production of all buses by White ended in 1953. In 1950 Autoridad de Transporte in San Juan, Puerto Rico, acquired a number of White Model 1144 buses. Pictured here is one of the buses at the Cleveland plant. Prior to 1946 private bus companies operated transit service in San Juan, and there were also streetcars operating until 1946. The Metropolitan Bus Company was formed in 1957 to operate bus service in San Juan.

One of the small cities operating Ford Transit Buses in the 1940s was Lincoln, Illinois, which had a population of 12,752. The bus line was called Lincoln Transit Lines. There were three of these Ford buses in the fleet in 1946. The Ford Transit Buses accommodated 27 passengers and had a 95-horsepower, 239-cubic-inch Ford V-8 engine mounted in the rear. Union City Body Company of Union City, Indiana, built bodies for the Ford Transit Buses. Approximately 12,500 Ford Transit Buses were built between 1939 and 1947.

The Twin Coach Model 44-D was introduced in 1946 along with other new Twin Coach models. The Model 44-D was a dual-engined bus that had two 180-horsepower Fageol Twin Coach underfloor gasoline engines. Approximately 30 transit systems purchased the Model 44-D. Cleveland (Ohio) Transit System acquired 10 in 1946, one of which is pictured here. Twin Coach also built the 44-S Model that had a single underfloor engine. Cleveland operated 145 of this model. Transit service came very early to Cleveland. Horse-drawn trolleys were reportedly in service in 1860. Streetcars came on all lines in 1901, and the first buses operated by Cleveland Railway Co. came in 1925. Trolley buses operated between 1936 and 1963. In 1975, The Greater Cleveland Transit Authority was formed.

The Twin Coach Co. introduced the Model 58-D Super Twin articulated bus in 1951. These buses had a vertical hinge in the joint, but they did not bend horizontally. They seated 58 passengers. There were 16 of these large buses built, and the Omaha and Council Bluffs (Nebraska) Street Railway Company purchased all but one of them. Omaha had its first transportation in 1868. Buses came into service by the Omaha and Council Bluffs Street Railway Company in 1925, although there were some buses in operation prior to that time. The Omaha and Council Bluffs Street Railway Company began in 1902 and continued for 70 years, when the Metro Area Transit Authority was established.

The Twin Coach Co. introduced new transit models in 1946. They featured a new body design with large side windows and a six-piece front wind-shield. An underfloor Fageol Twin Coach gasoline engine and Torsilastic suspension were featured. The Milwaukee (Wisconsin) Electric Railway & Transport Company, an important Twin Coach customer for many years, added the newest Twin Coaches to its fleet soon after World War II. Pictured here is a Model 38-SW that was added to the Milwaukee fleet in 1946. This particular bus was extra wide at 104 inches. Most buses at the time were 96 inches wide. Milwaukee had buses in service in the 1920s. Service operated privately, mainly under the name The Milwaukee Electric Railway and Transport Company, until 1975, when it became a county authority.

This bus, pictured in 1948, was in service for the Phoenix (Arizona) Transit System. It was built by Crown Body & Coach Manufacturing Co. of Los Angeles, California, and featured an underfloor engine. At the time, Crown special-ized in building fire trucks and school buses, but also built a limited number of transit buses. Phoenix had transit ser-vice in 1882, which was before Arizona became a state. In 1925 the municipally owned Phoenix Street Railway was organized. Streetcars were operated until 1948, at which time transit became private. Valley Transit and Metropolitan Lines were the primary companies serving the area. Transit in Phoenix returned to public ownership in 1972.

The United Electric Railways of Providence, Rhode Island, operated trolley bus service from 1931 to 1955. Rather than retire all of its trolley buses, some Pullman-Standard trolley buses were converted to diesel buses using Leyland diesel engines. These trolley buses ran until 1966 when the Rhode Island Public Transit Authority acquired United Transit, which was the new name for the transit system. One of the converted Pullman-Standard vehicles is pictured here. Providence had a large trolley bus operation, and in 1939 operated 310 trolley buses, most of which were Pullman-Standards.

Atlantic City, New Jersey, began operating jitney bus service in 1915. It has become an important part of the culture of the city and probably will continue for many years to come. At first, sedans were individually owned and operated for use in the jitney service. After World War II the jitney owners began operating van-type vehicles. Many of these new vehicles were called Metros, built by Metropolitan Body of Bridgeport, Connecticut, and were installed on International chassis. These Metros, one of which is pictured here on the Pacific Avenue route, lasted for many years. Later, a variety of vehicles went into service. The jitneys continue to be operated by individuals, but New Jersey Transit now funds the vehicles.

Marmon-Herrington Inc. of Indianapolis, Indiana, entered the bus-building business in 1945 with the introduction of a new trolley bus. In 1950, Marmon-Herrington got into the small bus business when the Ford Motor Company, which was building a small bus, decided to sell its transit business. The small bus had a postwar design and came in 27- and 31-passenger sizes. The buses continued to have six-cylinder Ford gasoline engines mounted in the rear. By the mid-1950s Marmon-Herrington discontinued building both trolley buses and buses. Overlake Transit Service of Seattle, Washington, operated one of the last Marmon-Herrington buses. Overlake began in 1938, and got its name because it operated service between Seattle and Mercer Island and Bellevue using a ferry across Lake Washington. When the Lake Washington Floating Bridge was built in 1940, through-bus service across the lake began. Overlake Transit became Metropolitan Transit Corporation, and in the early 1970s it was incorporated into Seattle Metro Transit.

Ford Motor Company had a long history of bus building. Prior to World War II Ford built many small 27-passenger buses, which were seen in most cities across the United States and Canada. They were sold primarily through Transit Bus Sales of Dearborn, Michigan. After World War II, Ford and Transit Bus went their separate ways, with both building different buses. Ford began selling a 27-passenger bus called the Metropolitan in 1945, but in 1950, Ford sold this business to Marmon-Herrington of Indianapolis, Indiana. Pictured here is one of the buses sold by Ford in 1948 to Les Autobus Jeromiens, Ltd., of St. Jerome, Quebec. This bus company began operating transit service in the St. Jerome area in 1945. It closed down 30 years later.

After World War II ACF-Brill Motors Co. in Philadelphia introduced new models of both intercity and city buses. One new model was the C-36. It had styling changes from prewar buses, but the C-36 continued to have underfloor Hall-Scott gasoline engines with some modifications to the accessories. Middlesex and Boston Street Railway of Waltham, Massachusetts, a very loyal ACF and ACF-Brill customer, purchased this Model C-36, and 21 others, in February 1947. The Middlesex and Boston Street Railway originated in 1915. Buses replaced streetcars in the area in 1931. The company was taken over by the Massachusetts Bay Transportation Authority in 1972.

Houston (Texas) Electric Co. was one of the first purchasers of the Model C-36 ACF-Brill bus. Ten were purchased in June 1946, shortly after production of the model began at the ACF-Brill plant in Philadelphia. These first Houston C-36 buses must have proven satisfactory, because in 1947, 46 more were added to the fleet. The one shown here is in downtown Houston. Houston Electric Co. began transit service in 1901, although other companies had streetcars earlier. The streetcars ended service in 1938. The name was changed to Houston Transit Co. in 1946. Then, in 1961, the company changed hands and became known as Rapid Transit Lines. The Metropolitan Transit Authority of Harris County became the public operator of transit service in the Houston area in 1974.

ACF-Brill Motors of Philadelphia, Pennsylvania, began producing a bus that was smaller than the buses the company had been building. The C-27 and C-31 models were introduced in 1948. It was an attempt by ACF-Brill to enter the small bus market, but by 1953 all ACF-Brill bus production ended. Approximately 500 C-27 and C-31 Brill buses were built. Grand Island, Nebraska, ordered two of the C-31 Brill buses in late 1949. The C-31 Brills had International 401-cubic-inch gasoline engines mounted in the rear. Grand Island Transit served Nebraska for only a few years. No company filled in following its demise.

Calgary (Alberta) Transit operated 30 Model C-36 CCF-Brill buses. The first 10 of the C-36 buses were delivered to Calgary Transit soon after CCF-Brill introduced the model to the Canadian market. The C-36 buses had a Hall-Scott underfloor gasoline engine. An AEC diesel engine was made available later. Calgary Transit succeeded Calgary Municipal Railway, which operated streetcars. Streetcar service began in 1909.

Port Arthur (Ontario) Utilities purchased this Can Car Model C-52 bus along with three others in 1959. These buses were among the last built in the Can Car factory in Fort William, Ontario, adjacent to Port Arthur. (Now both cities are combined and known as Thunder Bay.) Production of buses in Fort William began in 1945 under the name CCF-Brill. Production of Can Car buses moved to Montreal in 1960. The C-52 buses had AEC diesel underfloor engines and featured air suspension. Port Arthur also operated 10 CCF-Brill trolley buses, which were acquired in 1947, and served until 1971. Interestingly, Port Arthur operated only streetcars in transit service until 1945.

Most bus manufacturers introduced newly designed buses following World War II. Reo Motors Inc., of Lansing, Michigan, presented its 96-T Model buses in 1945. They carried the name Victory buses. One of the distinguishing features of the bus was the louver around the front destination sign. Behind was a channel that brought fresh air to the radiator, which was mounted above the Continental engine in the rear of the bus. Bodies were built by Meteor Motor Coach Co. in Piqua, Ohio, and mounted on a Reo chassis. This Reo Model 96 HT 33, and others, joined the Provincial Transport Company fleet in Montreal, Quebec, in 1946.

After working together for seven years, Ford Motor Company and Transit Buses parted company in 1948. Transit Buses and Union City Body Company, as the body builder, began marketing buses under the Transit Buses name. The new bus was a 31-seat model with a Checker Motors Co. chassis and a Continental engine mounted in the rear. The City of Detroit (Michigan) Department of Street Railways was the largest customer for the bus and placed an initial order for 300 units. Checker Motors of Kalamazoo, Michigan, purchased Transit Buses, Inc. in 1949 and built approximately 500 buses between 1951 and 1953. Detroit continued to favor this type of bus and eventually purchased 450, one of which is pictured here.

A number of small bus companies purchased Transit Bus buses. Mesaba Transportation Company of Hibbing, Minnesota, bought two Transit Buses in 1948, one of which is pictured here. Mesaba Transportation Company originated in 1914, and is considered the company from which Greyhound Lines had its start. Mesaba Transportation Company operated city service in Hibbing, as well as some intercity services, but the intercity service was eventually discontinued. Founders of the company left as it prospered, seeing new opportunities in expansion elsewhere. Andrew Anderson remained with Mesaba and was the president for many years. Mesaba Transportation Company ended city service in Hibbing in the 1980s and went out of business.

Many of the important transit bus manufacturers had closed their doors in the early 1950s, but Southern Coach Manufacturing Co. managed to continue. It, too, couldn't compete with GM and a few other bus manufacturers and finally ended most bus production in 1961. Birmingham (Alabama) Electric Company and its successor, Birmingham Transit Company, were important Southern customers. Birmingham ordered a total of 144 Southerns, including this Model S-45 DHC 45-passenger bus delivered in the spring of 1956. These buses had Cummins underfloor diesel engines. Birmingham operated streetcars until 1953. Trolley buses were also in service in Birmingham from 1947 to 1958. Public ownership of area transit came in 1971 with the establishment of the Birmingham-Jefferson County Transit Authority.

Baton Rouge (Louisiana) Bus Company succeeded the Baton Rouge Electric Company in 1938, two years after streetcar service ended. In August 1947 the Baton Rouge Bus Company acquired this Model F-31 bus from the Southern Coach Manufacturing Co. of Evergreen, Alabama. It was the last order of seven buses of this model for Baton Rouge. Southern Coach began supplying the Baton Rouge Bus Company with buses in 1946. There were 15 Model F-31s in the fleet. Later F-35, F-35M, S-41HF, and SH DHL model Southern buses were added. There were a total of 40 operated by the company. The Baton Rouge Bus Company continued until 1970, when Capital Transportation Corporation, a public company, became the operator.

Although Southern Coach Manufacturing Co. of Evergreen, Alabama, had its start in 1942, it was unable to begin its planned transit bus, the F-11, until 1945, when wartime restrictions were lifted. The company built approximately 1,400 F-11s before it ended all bus production in 1961. Companies in the southern states bought most Southern-built buses, although a few were exported. This Southern F-31 was one of four purchased by the Louisiana Power and Light Company of Gretna, Louisiana, in 1948. Westside Transit took over this bus operation in 1951.

San Antonio, Texas, had the distinction of being the first large United States city to become an all-bus city in 1932, when San Antonio had a population of 230,000. The system was operated by the San Antonio Public Service Co. There were fewer than 200 buses in service. The Public Service Co. sold the system to the San Antonio Transit Company in 1942. The city became the owner in 1959, operating as the San Antonio Transit System. The private transit company had a variety of bus makes, although Twin Coaches dominated the fleet. Fifty Southern Coach Model S-45-HF buses, one pictured here, came into the San Antonio fleet in 1954, the year the model was introduced. These buses had Fageol propane engines. VIA Metropolitan Transit became the publicly owned bus operation in 1978.

The Dallas (Texas) Railway & Terminal Company purchased 35 Model S 45 DHC buses from Southern Coach Manufacturing Company of Evergreen, Alabama, in 1955. One is pictured here. Dallas was the first company to add diesel Southern Model S 45 DHC buses to its fleet, acquiring 41 of them in 1953. When Dallas Railway & Terminal Co. became Dallas Transit in 1956, 55 Model S 50 DHC Southerns were purchased. They were the last Southerns built. Dallas had the largest fleet of diesel buses from Southern Coach.

FitzJohn Coach Company introduced new models of both city and intercity buses following World War II. The Model 310 Cityliner was the first postwar model and had a front-mounted Hercules JXD 6-cylinder gasoline engine. Blue Ribbon Lines of Ashland, Kentucky, purchased this Cityliner in 1945. Blue Ribbon Lines operated city service in the Ashland area beginning in 1936, when the Ohio Valley Electric Railway discontinued streetcar service. Blue Ribbon operated the bus service until 1959, when Ohio Valley Bus Company began operations.

In 1947 the FitzJohn Coach Company made some design changes to its Model 310 Cityliner. The Model 310 continued to have a front-mounted Hercules engine inside, but with a louvered front grille. Standee windows were also added. Simcoe (Ontario) Coach Lines acquired this FitzJohn Model 310 Cityliner in 1945. It ran on Simcoe service to Victoria, St. William, and Port Rowan. Canadian operators purchased many FitzJohn city buses, especially after FitzJohn Coach of Canada was established in Brantford, Ontario, in 1949.

Duquesne (Pennsylvania) Motor Coach Lines was one of the many suburban bus lines that served the Pittsburgh area. In addition to Duquesne, the company also served McKeesport, Mifflin, Homestead, and Munhall. Duquesne Motor Coach Lines began operating FitzJohn Cityliners in 1948, when four Model 310s were purchased. The previous year the design was changed, and featured an aluminum grille and standee windows. It had a 131-horsepower Hercules JXLD gasoline engine mounted inside in the front. In 1964, when the Port Authority of Allegheny County was established, Duquesne Motor Coach and other Pittsburgh suburban companies went into the new authority.

The FitzJohn Coach Company of Muskegon, Michigan, introduced the Cityliner FTG in 1950. It was a rear-engined bus with a body similar to the front-engined Cityliner, which was built in the late 1940s. FitzJohn also had a factory in Brantford, Ontario, and built the FTG model there for Canadian operators. Cape Breton Bus and Tram Co., Ltd., of Sydney, Nova Scotia, purchased four FitzJohn FTG buses in 1952. They were later sold to Pictou County Bus Services of New Glasgow, Nova Scotia. Bus service originated under the Pictou County Electric Company in 1926. The Irving Interests of New Brunswick purchased the company in 1987. *Paul Leger*

Chapter 7

Challenging Auto Competition

Ridership on city buses declined in the decades after World War II, from more than 23 billion in 1945, to 17 billion in 1950, and to just over 9 billion in 1960. The most significant factor for this decline was the emergence of the automobile. Automobile production was at an all-time high, and people began using their cars instead of public transportation. As a result, many bus builders quit producing transit vehicles.

In the years after the war transit systems continued their switch from streetcars to buses and trolleys. However, trolley buses were also falling out of favor, largely due to the tremendous expense of maintaining the overhead wires and infrastructure. Production of new trolley buses totaled just 224 in 1952, and, except in 1955 when 43 were built, no more were built during the remainder of the 1950s.

These two General Motors buses operated in Dubuque, Iowa, for more than 20 years. Bus 224 (in the foreground), a GM Model TDH 3206, was one of 10 purchased by the Interstate Power Company in 1946. Bus 240, a Model TDH 3207, was delivered to Interstate Power in 1947. The two models were similar. The Model TDH 3206 was built only in 1945 and 1946. The Model TDH 3207 was built only in 1947 and 1948. Interstate Power Company operated transit service in Dubuque for almost 50 years, beginning in 1924. In 1973 the Keyline Transit System was established. Dubuque had a long history of transit beginning in 1868 and for a time had an incline railway. Streetcars operated until 1932.

The Flxible Company survived the turbulent 1950s, when many manufacturers went out of business. In 1953 Flxible acquired Twin Coach's transit bus manufacturing operations. Flxible built Twin Coach buses for several years, mainly for the Chicago Transit Authority. The Chicago buses were propane powered. In 1964 Flxible purchased the Southern Coach Manufacturing Company and produced a new model, the Flxette, at its Evergreen, Alabama, plant.

Almost all of the buses sold in the United States were diesel powered. In 1956 the federal government initiated an antitrust suit claiming that GM Truck and Coach Division did not allow other manufacturers to purchase its popular two-cycle diesel engine. By the time GM began offering its engine to others, most of the other manufacturers had gone out of business.

CCF-Brill continued to produce transit buses at its plant in Fort William (now Thunder Bay), Ontario. In 1950 British AEC diesel engines were successfully used in CCF-Brill transit buses. In 1956 the CCF-Brill name was changed to Can Car. Can Car introduced a new TD-51 transit bus, but discontinued bus manufacturing altogether in 1962.

In 1959 General Motors introduced one of the most popular city buses of the 20th Century, the New Look. The New Look featured large side windows, an interesting eight-piece front windshield, and partial aluminum siding. The proven GM diesel engine, angle drive, automatic transmission, and air suspension were integral parts of the New Look. Air conditioning was also offered.

In addition to its United States business, GM had a large market in Canada with both transit and intercity GM buses being added to Canadian fleets. General Motors had begun building a non-air-conditioned New Look transit bus at its London, Ontario, plant in 1961.

Transit ridership continued to decline in the 1960s. This was reflected in the number of buses being built. In 1960 there were 2,806 transit buses built, but in 1969 the number had declined to 2,230. The total number of transit buses in service was just under 50,000 in 1965. That year about 6 billion passengers were carried on city buses.

Nineteen cities in the United States ended trolley bus operations by 1959, while trolley bus service continued in 14 Canadian cities. By the 1960s motorbuses were replacing trolley buses as well as the streetcars that were being operated by the troubled private transit companies.

Flxible introduced its own New Look transit bus in 1961. It had a GM diesel power plant and was purchased by many transit systems, including the Chicago Transit Authority.

GM continued to produce city buses. Beginning with the Model 4512 series, its buses were built with air suspension, which greatly improved the ride, and offered another benefit, ease of maintenance. In 1965 the name of the GM Diesel Division in Canada was changed to Detroit Diesel Division. Another division of the company, the Allison Division, built transmissions. General Motors had acquired the Allison Division in 1929.

Peoria (Illinois) Transportation Co. operated this GM Model TD 4007, which was acquired with 50 others in 1946. GM built this model with both diesel and gasoline engines. The first were built in 1944 and were replaced by the Models TDH and the TDM 4008 in 1946. Peoria had transit service prior to the beginning of the 20th Century. Between 1924 and 1946 power companies operated the services. When Peoria Transportation began serving Peoria, streetcar and trolley bus service ended. National City Lines had an interest in the company. When this picture was taken the name Peoria City Lines was used. In 1970 the Greater Peoria Mass Transit District took over the service.

Transportation service in Honolulu, Hawaii, began in the later part of the 19th Century. Some bus service began in 1915, but it wasn't until the Honolulu Rapid Transit Co. (HRT) became established that there was a commitment to having buses in service in the city. The bus fleet expanded and trolley buses were added in 1937. Four years later the streetcars were abandoned. During World War II HRT ridership increased dramatically to the extent that the existing bus fleet needed to be increased. Some Mack buses were acquired, including some on lease from the U.S. Navy. After World War II 100 new buses were purchased. Of those 100 new buses, 50 were GM TDH 4507 models. One of the first is pictured here. In 1971 HRT was taken over by the city and county of Honolulu. TL, Inc., which was made up of HRT management, was named to manage transportation in the Honolulu area.

The GM TD 4007 was one of the first 40-passenger diesel transit buses built after World War II. This one was delivered to the Union Street Railway Co. of New Bedford, Massachusetts. There were 25 TD 4007 buses in the Union Street Railway fleet. Street railway service in New Bedford began in 1874. Exactly 100 years later the Southeastern Massachusetts Transit Authority took over the Union Street Railway and began operating the buses in New Bedford as well as neighboring Fall River and other communities.

Greyhound Lines, the transcontinental bus system in the United States, also operated several large suburban transit systems, especially in California. In 1955, Pacific Greyhound purchased this GM TDM 4515 and 19 others for suburban service in the Los Angeles area. The Model TDM 4515 was one of the early transit buses to feature air suspension. The Model TDM 4515 was mainly a bus used in suburban services and most had mechanical transmissions (as noted by the M in the model number). It is interesting to note that Greyhound and a number of other large intercity bus companies had city bus subsidiaries. Some cities that had intercity bus companies operating their transit services included Charleston, West Virginia; Burlington, Vermont; Hagerstown, Maryland; Oklahoma City, Oklahoma; and others.

The Bi-State Development Agency was established in 1949 to operate transit service in the St. Louis, Missouri, area and bus service across the Mississippi River in Illinois. When Bi-State took over it acquired many of the buses of its predecessor, St. Louis Public Service Company. This GM Model TDH 4507 was one of the buses transferred. It was originally acquired in 1947. There were 250 of these buses operating in St. Louis. Most were purchased in 1947 or 1948. This particular bus was equipped with an air conditioning system, which was a retrofit on this model GM bus.

Beginning about 1915, Northern New Jersey had jitney services operated by individuals. The New Jersey Public Utilities Commission began regulating them and required buses to be operated on specific routes by the jitney owners. As a result, there were many buses owned individually or by small bus companies. There were a variety of bus makes and liveries. The Hudson County Boulevard was one route. Rialto Bus Company of Union City, New Jersey, had this GM TGM in its boulevard service in 1947. The State of New Jersey took over transit operations, but many individual bus owners and companies continued. The buses have been subsidized. The number on the side of this bus, B-139, is also the permit number.

Jamaica Buses, Inc., of Jamaica, New York, purchased 17 GM TDH 5106 buses in the 1950s. This one was part of an order in 1955. The Model TDH 5106 was one of the first transit models to feature air suspension. Jamaica Buses, which began in 1931, operated buses in the southeastern area of Queens County and the southwestern area of Nassau County in metropolitan New York City. Several private bus companies in the area, including Command Bus Company, Triboro Coach Corporation, and Green Bus Lines, operated similar service and for many years shared common ownership. These companies provided service in the New York City area as private companies through the end of the 20th Century.

Chicago (Illinois) Motor Coach Company took delivery of 100 GM TDH 5502 buses in 1948. These 42-foot, 55-passenger buses were acquired to replace the Model 720 double-deck buses that had been in service for 10 years. The new buses had GM six-cylinder diesel engines and hydraulic "V" drives. Following the acquisition of these buses, Chicago Motor Coach Company purchased 100 GM Model TDH 5103 buses and eight Mack C-550T buses in 1950 and 1951. In 1952, after 35 years of service in Chicago, the Chicago Motor Coach Company became a part of the Chicago Transit Authority.

The bus pictured here is a GM Model TDH 3610 built in 1948. The first buses of this model were introduced in 1946 and continued in production for two more years. This particular bus was in the Pontiac (Michigan) City Lines fleet for a number of years. National City Lines owned Pontiac City Lines, as well as many other bus companies. National City Lines also operated Montgomery (Alabama) City Lines, which also had the same Model TDH 3610 GM buses. It was on this same kind of bus that Rosa Parks began the civil rights protests that lead to the Supreme Court ruling that segregation of public transportation was unconstitutional. The Montgomery City Lines bus, called the Rosa Parks Bus, has been rescued and restored, and is now in the Henry Ford Museum in Dearborn, Michigan.

Twin City Lines operated transit service in the Minneapolis and St. Paul areas. Streetcars dominated service prior to 1950. There were only a few buses in the fleet, mainly Mack buses. In the early 1950s new management came on board and it was decided to convert to an all-bus system. Even postwar PCC streetcars were discontinued. Although some Macks were used for replacement of the streetcars, most of the buses used by the new Twin City Lines system were GM TDH 5103 52-passenger buses, one of which is pictured here. It was obtained in an order placed in 1952 for more than 100 of this model. More GM large buses were added in the following years. All streetcar service in the area ended in 1954.

New Orleans (Louisiana) Public Service, Inc. favored buses manufactured by White Motor Company in the 1940s and operated approximately 350 units in its fleet. In 1945 the company's first 100 GM buses were acquired. By 1954 the company's fleet was dominated with buses purchased from General Motors, all of which were Model TDH 5105 units. Seen in this picture traveling on the Florida route through the French Quarter is one of the GM buses added in 1957. New Orleans was operating three modes of vehicles at the time; streetcars, trolley buses, and buses. Trolley bus service ended in 1967. It is interesting to note that New Orleans was one of the last large cities to have a private transit system, although there were subsidies. The Regional Transit Authority was formed in June 1983.

Reo Motors Inc., of Lansing, Michigan, used the name Flying Cloud for a new bus design in 1948. The Mason City (Iowa) Motor Coach Company had three Reo Flying Cloud buses, each slightly different. Mason City Motor Coach Company was a short-lived city bus company. After building approximately 100 of the new buses Reo found it could not compete with buses produced by other manufacturers. The company discontinued building all commercial buses by 1949.

The Erie (Pennsylvania) Coach Company acquired 10 of these buses in 1960. They had Marmon-Herrington chassis with bodies from a little-known company named Oneida. In 1967 Erie Coach Company, which began in 1925, ceased operations, and the Erie Metropolitan Transit Authority was formed. Erie Coach Company had operated a variety of bus types, including Transit Buses, Yellow Coaches, Whites, Fords, Blue Birds, and Macks.

The Metropolitan Suburban Bus Authority on Long Island, New York, was formed in 1973. It took over a number of private transit systems that had been servicing the area for many years. There had been many private bus lines on Long Island, which provided local service, as well as making connections with the Long Island Railroad for commuters who traveled into New York City. Hempstead Bus Company was one of the bus companies that served Long Island. It operated a number of Mack C-41GT buses, the first being added in 1948. One of the 32 Hempstead Mack buses is pictured here.

This Mack C-37 T was one of 50 delivered to the International Railway Company (IRC) of Buffalo, New York, in October 1949. Mack C-37 and C-33 models were introduced in 1948. Their production lasted less than five years. International Railway Company was formed late in the 19th Century. In 1902 there was a consolidation of seven or eight transit companies in the Buffalo area. Buffalo Traction Company was the largest, but the International Railway Company name was adopted. In 1926 buses began service in Buffalo. In 1950 IRC reorganized as Niagara Frontier Transit. Niagara Frontier Metro System, a public agency, was established in 1974.

Bus manufacturers throughout the United States were discontinuing building buses by the mid-1950s. However, Mack carried on and even presented new models. In 1959 Mack made a styling change to the front of the model that was being produced at the time, and it was referred to as the Model C-47-DT. Denver (Colorado) Tramways Co. acquired 24 of these buses in 1959. They were the first Macks acquired by Denver in 20 years.

San Francisco (California) Municipal Railway (MUNI) purchased 70 C-49 buses from Mack in 1959-60. One is pictured here. Mack began building the C-49 in 1954 and continued building them until 1960 when, after more than a half century of bus manufacturing, Mack went out of the transit-bus building business. MUNI, along with the New York City Transit System and Niagara Frontier Transit System of Buffalo, New York, were the largest users of postwar Mack buses. MUNI operated many of the Mack buses through a lease arrangement with Mack. San Francisco Municipal Railway became a transit operator in San Francisco in 1912. At the time, the Market Street Railway also provided service. MUNI acquired the Market Street Railway in 1944.

Two of the large C-49 Mack buses that were acquired by the San Francisco Municipal Railway in 1959-60 were reduced in size at MUNI's 24th and Utah Division shops. This was done so that the buses could operate the Coit-Tower Line, which had very narrow streets. Note that the bus had been equipped with a special energy absorption bumper. This type of bumper was later modified and became standard on transit buses everywhere.

Excel Coach Lines of Kenora, Ontario, had its start in 1934, serving the areas of the small city of Kenora on the large Lake of the Woods and in neighboring Keewatin. In addition to the urban service Excel Coach Lines operated charter, school bus, and intercity service. In 1950 this Prevost city bus was purchased. It featured a Hercules JXLD 6-cylinder rear-mounted engine. Prevost Car, Inc. began building intercity buses in 1924. Intercity buses were Prevost's primary focus, but there was a short period in the 1950s when city buses were also built.

Pictured is a Beaver Model B-25-PT sold to Valley Transit Company (VTC) of Harlingen, Texas, in 1953. This model joined 16 other postwar Beaver Model B-25-PT buses in the VTC fleet. This was the last Beaver bus acquired by Valley Transit. Valley Transit Company originated in 1941. It began by operating bus service to communities in the Rio Grande Valley. Valley Transit also had city services and a route between McAllen, Texas, and Reynosa, Mexico. It is believed to be the first company to receive authority to cross the Mexican border with regular bus service. The city service of VTC was one of the only city bus services in the United States to operate with a subsidy well into the 1980s. Today, VTC is a part of Greyhound Lines.

Western Flyer Coach Ltd., of Winnipeg, Manitoba, was well known in Canada for the front-engined intercity buses it built from the late 1930s through the 1950s. A Model C was first produced in 1947, but most went to Canadian government agencies or for sightseeing service. The only C-33 Model Western Flyer built, a true city bus, was this one that was delivered in 1950 to Northern Bus Lines in Flin Flon, Manitoba. Northern Bus Lines first operated city bus service in Flin Flon for the Hudson Bay Mining and Smelter Company under contract, and then assumed the city service in 1952. Flin Flon is a mining community located on a very rocky hill on the Manitoba-Saskatchewan border.

The General American Aerocoach Co. of East Chicago, Indiana, first entered the bus-building business with intercity buses in 1940. In 1948 the company, while still building intercity buses, launched a city-bus venture. Two models were offered; one was a 36-passenger bus, and the other seated 45 passengers. Very few were sold. Indiana Railroad of Indianapolis, Indiana, a division of the Wesson Co., acquired a small fleet of these buses in 1949 and used them primarily on a service between Indianapolis and Fort Benjamin Harrison. Aerocoach ended all of its bus-building activity in 1952. *Motor Bus Society*

After World War II, Transit Buses, Inc. of Dearborn, Michigan, which was the sales organization for the Ford Transit Buses, parted company with Ford, as did Union City Body Company. Transit Buses and Union City Body then introduced a new bus, called the Transit Bus, in 1948. Union City built the bodies and Checker Motors Corporation of Kalamazoo, Michigan, built the chassis. A Continental gasoline engine was mounted in the rear. The Detroit (Michigan) Department of Street Railways ordered 300 of these buses in 1949, one of which is pictured here. This was Transit Bus's largest order.

Cook Street Bus Company of Waterbury, Connecticut, purchased this bus from Transit Buses in late 1952. At the time, Checker Motors of Kalamazoo, Michigan, was building the bus. The Detroit Department of Street Railways placed a large order for the Checker-built Transit Bus, but few other operators acquired this model. The last ones were built in 1953. Cook Street Bus Company was a small company, which had been in bus service since the 1930s. It operated in the north part of the city of Waterbury.

The Flxible Company of Loudonville, Ohio, took over the building of Twin Coach transit buses in 1952. They were built in Loudonville under the name Flxible-Twin Coach. Chicago (Illinois) Transit Authority acquired 900 Flxible-Twin Coach Model FT2-P-40, 54-passenger buses between 1951 and 1958. They were all propane powered. The bus pictured here was delivered in 1954. During that time surface streetcars of the Chicago Transit Authority were discontinued. Trolley buses remained in Chicago until 1973.

Chapter 8

Private Transit Ends

The 1950s marked the beginning of profound changes in the culture of the United States. Up to that time racial segregation was the norm in the South. On buses, black passengers were not allowed to sit in any row in front of white passengers. If a white person boarded a bus and there were no seats available, the black passengers were required to move further back on the bus to allow the white person a seat in front of them. On December 1, 1955, a woman named Rosa Parks refused to give up her seat on a General Motors TDH 3610 transit bus in Montgomery, Alabama. Mrs. Parks was jailed for her refusal. Her courageous stand spurred boycotts of transit systems in Tuscaloosa, Birmingham, and other cities, and helped launch the American civil rights movement.

Most city transit systems in the early 1950s were under private ownership. Only a few cities had publicly owned systems, including Seattle, San Francisco, and Detroit. In the mid- to late-1950s there was a quick changeover from private to public ownership of many

The Connecticut Company, owned by the New York, New Haven, and Hartford Railroad, operated considerable local transit service in Connecticut, including Hartford, New Haven, and other larger cities in the state. It had its beginnings in the early part of the 20th Century and was the dominant provider of bus services in Connecticut until 1976, when the publicly owned Connecticut Transit came into existence. In 1967 this GM Model TDH 5303 and 33 others joined the Connecticut Company fleet. This Model 5303 was one of the first air-conditioned buses in transit service in Connecticut.

city systems. By 1979 only a few privately operated transit systems remained in the United States.

With the growth of the suburbs in the 1950s, providing suburban bus service had proven profitable for private companies such as Greyhound Lines in San Francisco, Los Angeles, Seattle, Detroit, Buffalo, Pittsburgh, and other areas. However, the increase in automobile use and rising labor costs decreased the profits from suburban services drastically, and Greyhound and other private companies finally discontinued their suburban services. Eventually, private suburban services were ended nearly everywhere. The creation of Bay Area Rapid Transit, Golden Gate Transit, and San Mateo County Transit District contributed to the demise of privately operated service in those areas. American Transit Corporation, which owned 38 bus operations in the late 1960s, took over the suburban services in Detroit and Seattle.

In the 1960s National City Lines disposed of some of the large city transit systems in which it had an interest, but continued to own bus systems in 21 cities. In 1961 the company began offering a new service, contract management, to the many newly formed public transit systems. A city could sign a contract with National City Lines for the complete management of its system at a fixed price for a certain period. Its first management contract was with Miami-Dade Transit in Florida. American Transit Corporation became involved in management services, as well. Another management service company, McDonald Transit Corporation, was founded in 1972.

During the 1960s and 1970s transit management services offered the new systems valuable expertise in operating a transit system. Over the years, however, most transit agencies were able to begin operating their own systems. This was possible partly because of the growing availability of training in transit operations, which had not been available in the early days. A number of universities began offering courses in transit education, notably Indiana University, Northwestern University, and a few others. These courses of study gave students an opportunity to follow a career in transit and helped give transit agencies the expertise to operate on their own.

American Transit Enterprises was a holding company. By 1967 it owned some 18 transit companies. Its head, David Ringo, recognized the advantage of management services and established ATE Management and Service Corporation. In the late 1970s ATE entered into a joint venture in Saudi Arabia. ATE provided the organization and management of a public transportation system for the Saudi Public Transport Company. The venture lasted just five years, and ended in 1984.

In Canada, Toronto, Ontario, established a new transit system, GO (Government of Ontario) Transit in 1967. It involved a number of commuter routes serving the Toronto metropolitan area. The agency also operated a large fleet of buses in commuter service and GO Transit commuter trains on some routes.

General Motors presented four newly designed bus models in 1959. They were referred to as "New Look" buses. The Los Angeles (California) Metropolitan Transportation Authority was one of the first transit systems to add the new models to its fleet. It chose the Model TDH 5301 and ordered 75 units in December 1959. This order was followed by additional orders in 1960 and 1961 amounting to more than 200 of the New Look buses. One of the first to see service in the Los Angeles area is pictured here. It is seen in a special transit stop in a pocket off a freeway. Many other cities had similar freeway transit stops. Transit began in Los Angeles circa 1874. Buses were in service in the early part of the 20th Century. The Los Angeles area began public transit operations in 1958.

Philadelphia (Pennsylvania) Transportation Co. succeeded the Philadelphia Rapid Transit Co. in 1940. The municipal company operated the buses as well as streetcars, heavy rail, and trolley buses. Southeastern Pennsylvania Transportation Authority, a regional transportation system, was established in 1968. When it was formed, buses of the Philadelphia Transportation Co. were acquired. There were a number of General Motors New Look buses in the fleet at that time, including the GM TDH 5305 pictured here, which was one of 50 purchased in 1963. Also that year, 43 Model TDH 5304 were added, along with some suburban Model SDM 5302 buses.

General Motors began building transit and intercity buses in Canada in 1961 under the Diesel Division name. Initially the factory was in London, Ontario. The St. John's (Newfoundland) Transportation Commission, which was established in 1958, ordered five Diesel Division Model TDH 4517 buses in 1962. In 1965, 10 Model TDH 4519 buses were acquired, followed by 25 similar buses in 1971. The Canadian-built General Motors buses were similar to those built in the United States, but lacked air conditioning. St. John's had a street railway in 1900, and streetcars continued operating there until 1948. Transit was by private bus operators until 1958. Trolley buses were even considered at one time, but the plan never materialized.

South Suburban Safeway Lines of Harvey, Illinois, was one of the important suburban bus companies in the Chicago area. It operated from various suburban communities into downtown Chicago, and also operated local service in the suburban area. In 1960, soon after General Motors introduced the New Look bus series, South Suburban Safeway Lines purchased three GM Model TDH 5301 buses, one of which is pictured here. These GM buses had the new Detroit Diesel 8V-71 diesel engine. The Chicago south suburban area had electric streetcars beginning in 1893. Bus services began over some routes in 1924. South Suburban Safeway Lines began in 1933 and continued for 50 years, after which Chicago's Regional Transportation Authority acquired it. Two years later it became a part of Pace South Division.

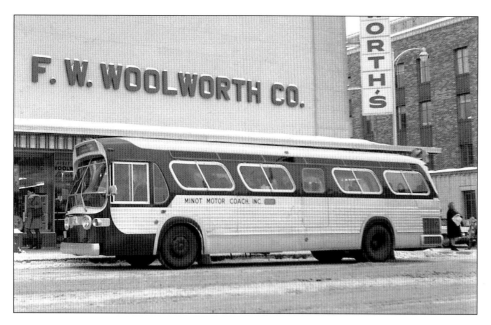

Minot, North Dakota, a city with a population of 35,000, had two city bus companies after World War II. One of the companies was Minot Motor Coach, Inc., which purchased this GM Model T6H 4561 bus in July 1968. Minot Motor Coach was privately operated until the City of Minot became the operator of transit service in the city in 1975.

A second of two city bus services operating in Minot, North Dakota, was the Yellow Bus Company. Pictured is the GM TDH 3501 that was acquired in October 1967. In the mid-1960s, after General Motors introduced the New Look 45- and 53-passenger models, there wasn't a smaller 35-passenger bus built by General Motors. As a result, the Model 3501 was introduced, using the "old look" body style. Many small bus companies, especially in Canada, purchased this model.

Steam used to power trains had originated early in the 19th Century, and there were even examples of steam-powered road vehicles. Some buses in service in Great Britain in the early 20th Century were steam powered. There were a number of experiments in the United States to build and market buses powered by steam, but they never came into mass production. In early 1969 the United States Department of Transportation began funding a program with the California State Assembly to develop a steam-powered bus. Several companies expressed interest in the program, including the San Francisco Municipal Railway and AC Transit of Oakland, California. Pictured is a GM Model TDH 5301 of AC Transit, one of the buses completed with steam power, which underwent testing. William M. Brobeck & Associates developed the bus. This bus and others that were involved proved unsuccessful and the steam bus program was eventually laid to rest.

Philadelphia Suburban Transportation Co. of Upper Darby, Pennsylvania, operated suburban rail service from Philadelphia to the city's western suburbs. The company also had a sizable bus operation known as Aronimink Transportation Company. Both the interurban trains and buses used the name Red Arrow Lines. In 1967 management decided to run a test on a bus, a GM New Look model that could travel on rails as well as on the streets and highways. Fairmont (Minnesota) Railway Motors equipped this bus with a rail device in front of the rear wheels. The bus was called the Hy-Rail. The concept was to have the bus avoid congestion and operate on rails to suburban locations and then use the streets, thereby giving seamless transportation to the passengers.

The New Look transit style by General Motors was introduced on a 29-foot bus model in 1969. It was offered with either a GM 478 Toro-Flow II diesel engine or a GM 351 V-8 gasoline engine. Most were sold with diesel engines. The basic models were the TDH 3301 and the TDH 3302. Seating capacity was 33 passengers. In the five years the buses were built approximately 500 were sold. Springfield (Missouri) City Utilities was one of the first bus systems to operate the Model 3301. Three were delivered in November 1969 and two more were added in 1971. Springfield Traction Company operated transit service in Springfield until 1945 when the municipal City Utilities acquired the transit service, which it has operated ever since.

Pictured is the first newly designed transit bus introduced by The Flxible Company in 1961. It had a six-piece windshield and four-piece side windows. This bus and 300 similar buses were delivered to the Chicago (Illinois) Transit Authority in 1961. The Flxible Company began producing city buses when it acquired the rights from the Twin Coach Company in 1953. The Flxible and Twin Coach emblem appeared on this bus. The two emblems were used for a number of years.

New York City Transit Authority of Brooklyn, New York, was the operator of approximately 660 New Look transit buses from The Flxible Company of Loudonville, Ohio, in the early 1970s. One of the first is pictured here. These 40-foot buses seated 53 passengers. A Detroit Diesel 6V-71 diesel engine was used in these Flxible buses. There were more than 13,000 of this model built. In 1970 Rohr Industries of Chula Vista, California, acquired The Flxible Company. A new factory was built in 1974 to produce Flxible transit buses.

The Montreal (Quebec) Transportation Commission operated the largest fleet of the Can Car Model TD-51 buses, which were introduced in 1960, along with a smaller model, the TD-43. Montreal had 50 of the Model TD-51 buses. An AEC diesel engine mounted in the rear was used, but at first it had a number of problems. The British engine manufacturer eventually corrected these problems. Canada's bus operators at the time were beginning to acquire General Motors transit buses, which were becoming popular in Canada. Production ended after 689 of the new Can Car buses were built. Montreal had a large fleet of previous Can Car models, plus a number of other makes.

In 1960 Can Car of Montreal, Quebec, decided to introduce an entirely new bus design with its T-43 and T-51 models. Both models had AEC Model A 690 diesel engines mounted in the rear, but the engines in these buses proved to be unsatisfactory. The new buses had good potential, but there was new competition from General Motors. The last Can Car buses were delivered in 1962. London (Ontario) Transportation Commission was one of 11 Canadian companies that purchased the two models. London had 10 T-43 models, one of which is pictured here. London, Ontario, has a rich transit history. Buses were first introduced there in 1923. The London Street Railway Company had a 75-year history up to 1950. The London Transportation Commission was the transit operator at that time and became known as the London Transit Commission.

The Metropolitan Corporation of Greater Winnipeg (Manitoba) Transit Department purchased 15 Model MAR 750 L buses in 1966 from the Japanese bus manufacturer Mitsubishi Heavy Industries. The buses accommodated 51 passengers and featured 6-cylinder diesel engines. They operated in transit service in Winnipeg for several years. No further Japanese buses were purchased for Winnipeg. At one time there were about 282 buses in the Winnipeg transit fleet. Most were CCF-Brill and Flxible Twin Coach buses. There were also 140 trolley buses.

Canadian cities had operated a number of buses built in England in the 1930s, and even following World War II there were a few English-built buses purchased. In 1964, Edmonton (Alberta) Transit bought three 45-passenger Japanese-built Model GRA 110 Nissan buses. These buses were followed by 10 more of the same type in 1966. The Nissan bus pictured here is one of the first ones in the Edmonton fleet. They proved to be unsatisfactory and were retired after only a few years. No more Japanese-built buses where purchased by Edmonton Transit. Edmonton had its first transit in 1908, operated by the Edmonton Radial Railway Co. In 1936 it became the Edmonton Transportation System. The first buses entered service in Edmonton in 1932, and two years later the first trolley buses were introduced.

Western Flyer Coach, Ltd. presented the 700 Series city transit buses to Winnipeg, Manitoba, in 1967. Metro Transit of the Metropolitan Corporation of Greater Winnipeg acquired the first one of this model Western Flyer. Approximately 150 of these buses were in operation in Winnipeg by the end of 1969. The Model D700 Western Flyer had a Detroit Diesel 6V-71N engine. Particular attention was given to special thick insulation in the body to keep the bus cool in the summer and warm in the winter. Western Flyer Coach became Flyer Industries in 1971.

The Coachette Company of Dallas, Texas, began selling small buses in 1954. The buses were built on Ford chassis and accommodated 21 to 31 passengers. Ward Body Company of Austin, Texas, built the bodies until 1967, and then American Body Company of Grand Prairie, Texas, built them until Coachette discontinued selling buses. A slanted front on the buses gave way to a flat-front design in 1956. A 33-passenger 1961 model was a demonstrator at first, and eventually ended up in Canada. The 1961 model was operated by the Glace Bay (Nova Scotia) Bus Co. and then went into service for Moncton (New Brunswick) Transit, Ltd. It ended its days in 1972.

Schuylkill Valley Lines of Norristown, Pennsylvania, succeeded Schuylkill Valley Transit Company after streetcars were discontinued in 1933. Schuylkill operated in a suburban area northwest of Philadelphia. In 1962 it was operating this Divco-Wayne Bantam Transit Bus. The Wayne Corporation of Richmond, Indiana, was a school bus builder that originated in 1931, but also built a few transit and other type buses. In 1959, The Divco Corporation of Detroit, Michigan, purchased Wayne, and it was then called Divco-Wayne Corporation. Divco also built small delivery vans. When Divco joined with Wayne, this small bus, built on a forward-control Divco chassis, was introduced. Only a few were ever built.

Telebus was a special door-to-door bus service inaugurated by the Regina (Saskatchewan) Transit System in 1972. The concept was for a small bus to circulate in a designated area and respond to telephone calls from a central dispatcher through a radio, and then pick up passengers at or near their doorstep. Passengers could call the dispatch center and receive bus service in a reasonable amount of time. They could also reserve a bus to stop in advance, and even have a standard daily pick-up arranged. The Telebus vehicles would go to a transfer point and the passengers would transfer to regularly scheduled fixed-route buses. The Regina Transit System operated one 25-passenger Unibus and two Dodge vans in this service. Unibus Corporation, a division of Bus Sales of Canada of Malton, Ontario, sold Unibuses with Van Hool bodies and Ford chassis.

The Flxible Company introduced a small 19-passenger bus in 1965. The new bus was known as the Flxette. It was built in a factory in Evergreen, Alabama, which had previously built Southern transit buses. The Flxette was built on a Ford chassis. Mansfield (Ohio) Bus Lines purchased the first four Flxette buses when it started a new service in the city. The new operator, formerly a taxi company, added several more Flxettes as patronage increased.

Minibus, Inc. of Pico Rivers, California, began producing small buses for shuttle services, mainly in downtown sections of cities, in 1967. The Detroit Department of Street Railways operated the Minibus pictured here in downtown Detroit, Michigan, in 1967. The standard Minibus seated from 19 to 23 passengers and was powered by a Dodge engine. A dual-fuel system was available, using either diesel fuel or liquefied petroleum gas. The Minibus company built a variety of concepts for special bus transportation, including streetcar designs and bus trains, especially for amusement parks.

Key West (Florida) Transit Authority operated seven of these Highway Products (Twin Coach) Model T31-TO buses in 1974. They joined two similar T-24 Highway Products buses which were added in 1970. The newer buses had two doors, with the rear door positioned behind the rear wheels. This bus also had a large space for advertising above the windows. The large signs attracted advertising revenue. Key West had transit with streetcars from 1891 until 1926, after which there was no transit service. After World War II numerous private companies tried transit in Key West prior to the public authority, which was formed in the early 1970s.

Chapter 9

Government Funding Begins

As the number of passengers on transit buses continued to decline efforts were made to stimulate ridership. Agencies tried to upgrade their equipment in order to make buses more comfortable and more attractive to riders. New buses were being added, often with considerable publicity. Bus designs were streamlined to make them look more modern and less like the old box-type buses of earlier days. Fabric seats and attractive paint schemes were adopted, and air conditioning for city buses was becoming more common.

Weekly and monthly pass systems were established by many systems in order to make it easier for passengers to board. As fares rose during the 1970s fare boxes were built to accept dollar bills, and later, even accepted credit card-like devices known as Smart Cards.

The Flxible Company of Loudonville, Ohio, had been building city buses with a new design for 10 years when it obtained an order for six 40-passenger buses from the Southern California Rapid Transit District of Los Angeles. This one was delivered in 1973. By the end of 1975 Southern California Rapid Transit had approximately 250 of these buses in its fleet. At the time, transit systems were receiving subsidies and renewing their fleets. Even though the low-bid process was in effect, Flxible managed to secure some large orders. The Southern California Rapid Transit District was formed in 1964.

The United States government was becoming more influential in setting policy and providing funding for the nation's transportation system. In 1956 the Federal Highway Act was signed, launching construction of the nation's interstate highway system. While new highway building was a boon to long-distance bus travel, it also helped urban transit systems link with commuters by offering express bus services to suburban areas.

In 1961 the federal government authorized $25 million for mass transportation demonstration projects as part of the Housing Act. Mass transportation planning and loans for capital improvements were also authorized.

President Lyndon Johnson signed the Urban Mass Transportation Act of 1964, which authorized low-interest loans and capital grants to public organizations or to private enterprise in conjunction with and through public organizations. At first the grants covered up to two-thirds of the costs of facilities and equipment.

Also, in 1964, the Department of Transportation (DOT) became a cabinet-level agency of the government. Alan Boyd was named its first secretary. In 1968 the Urban Transportation Administration was brought from the Department of Housing and Urban Development into the DOT and became known as the Urban Mass Transportation Administration.

The federal government wanted fares to remain stable, service to be expanded, and ridership to be increased, but transit was never a strong priority in any election. Changes in administrations, not only in the federal government but also the states and cities, brought differing support to transit. Although some funding came through the Highway Trust Fund, there was no dedicated funding source for transit-related programs. Ongoing funding was subject to periodic renewal, and a great deal of lobbying was necessary to convince policy makers of the value of good transit service, and to obtain the needed funding.

The situation became progressively more complicated as more and more requests for transit projects were made. Originally, most transit funding requests came from the big cities, but soon everyone wanted a piece of the pie. Rural areas, intercity bus operators, Amtrak, and others felt they deserved part of the money spent for transportation. In addition, the highway lobby was very strong in its efforts to obtain funding to build and maintain roads. Special interest groups were also requesting funds, particularly the elderly and disabled, who were demanding full accessibility to transit.

The Flxible Company began building New Look transit buses in 1960. The first buses were 40-foot models, followed by 35-foot buses. The HD-31 heavy-duty small bus was introduced in 1975. The Joliet (Illinois) Mass Transit District took delivery of 14 of these new Flxible buses in 1975. They had Detroit Diesel 6V-71 diesel engines. Early HELP bumpers designed by Firestone were installed. The HELP bumpers were an innovation that gave the bus added protection from damage in the event of an accident. Joliet Mass Transit District was established in 1970. It became a part of a regional transportation service area of Chicago called Pace. It was named Pace Heritage Division and is one of eight divisions. It continues to be based in Joliet.

The need for transit funding continued to grow as the number of publicly owned transit systems was steadily increasing. Important transportation legislation was enacted throughout the 1970s, including the Mass Transportation Assistance Act of 1970, the Federal Aid Highway Act of 1973, the National Mass Transportation Assistance Act of 1974, and the Surface Transportation Act of 1978.

States, cities, and other local governments were becoming more involved in transit and were being called upon to assist with transit funding. Regional transit authorities were being authorized. Each level of government had taxing power, providing more support to transit systems. One state, Rhode Island, had a statewide transit system. Although there had been some state departments of transportation earlier, more were eventually established.

In 1971 the state of New Jersey became the owner and operator of services provided by the Public Service Coordinated Transport Co. The agency was renamed

Transport of New Jersey in 1980. Many of the pioneer bus associations formed by the independent bus operators continued but the state purchased the buses to be operated by the independents. Surviving associations include the Bergen Avenue Bus Owners, South Hudson County Boulevard Bus Owners, Central Avenue Bus Owners, and others. Some associations became corporations and continued to operate independently.

In the 1960s and 1970s universities and colleges in the United States were experiencing growing enrollment. The addition of many new buildings increased the size of the various campuses, and spawned a new type of transit service, the campus bus service. One of the first to have a campus bus service was The Ohio State University in Columbus. Two other early campus bus services were at Kent State University in Kent, Ohio, and the University of Georgia in Athens.

Some universities were in very small communities, such as the University of Massachusetts in Amherst, the University of Connecticut in Storrs, and Northern Illinois University in De Kalb. There had been no urban service previously in those communities; therefore, the communities were also served when campus bus services were established.

The University of California at Davis originated a unique campus bus service. Double-deck buses from England were acquired to operate on the campus routes. The students liked these buses.

The oil crisis in 1973 and 1974 had an effect on the city bus industry, even though transit agencies themselves did not suffer from fuel shortages. The government recognized the importance of both transit and intercity bus service, and made it possible for the industry to obtain fuel. However, the fuel shortage resulted in dramatic fuel price increases, which in turn lead to fare increases. Despite rising fares, ridership also went up in some cases, as private automobile owners, finding it difficult to get fuel for their cars, turned to the bus for transportation. Even though oil shipments eventually increased, the world's way of thinking was changed forever. Measures were taken to reduce fuel consumption, spurring research on more efficient engines and alternative fuels.

The federal government set up a program to introduce a new bus design and encouraged the three major manufacturers at that time, GMC Truck and Coach Division, AM General, and Rohr Flxible, to design a new bus known as the Transbus. Each company built a prototype model, but the program was unsuccessful and the buses were scrapped. However, modified bus designs by GMC Truck and Coach and The Flxible Company followed.

GMC Truck and Coach introduced a new bus design in 1977, the Rapid Transit Series (RTS) Advanced Design Bus (ADB). The RTS had many new features and was a definite departure from GMC's New Look design of the 1950s.

Grumman Allied Industries of Garden City, New York, acquired the J. B. Olson Corporation, maker of aluminum-alloy truck bodies, in 1963. New federal subsidies for bus service caused heightened demand for small buses. As a result, Grumman launched a 19-passenger small bus in 1970. It was mounted on a choice of chassis, including Ford, Chevrolet, and others. The aluminum bodies were advertised to last 15 to 20 years. Regional Transit Services of Rochester, New York, operated this Grumman bus in a Dial-a-Bus service called PERT in a suburban area of Rochester. The Grumman Corporation purchased The Flxible Company in 1978 and began building large Flxible transit buses. Small bus building activity eventually ended.

AM General became a bus-building company in the United States in 1974. At first, the company had a working arrangement with Flyer Industries in Winnipeg, Manitoba, to build the bodies for AM General buses. The front of the bus and the section above the belt was an AM General design, but the section below the belt and the drive train was a Flyer Industries product. The buses came in 35- and 40-foot lengths and used Detroit Diesel 8V-71 or 6V-71 diesel engines. Many transit systems had AM General buses in their fleets in the 1970s. The Twin Cities Area Metropolitan Transit Commission, serving the Minnesota cities of Minneapolis and St. Paul, had approximately 230 Model 10240B AM General buses. One of the Commission's buses is pictured here. The bus was named "The Oughta Mobile" and featured advertising used by the Commission to increase ridership.

Missoula, Montana, began the Missoula Urban Transportation District in 1977. It devoted considerable attention to attracting passengers. A mountain lion was presented as a mascot and was pictured on timetables and other printed publicity. The system adapted the name, The Mountain Line. In 1979, four Orion Model 01-501 30-foot transit buses were purchased to supplement the small O-309D Mercedes-Benz buses that were in operation. Orion buses were first introduced in 1976 and were sold in Canada by Ontario Bus Industries of Mississauga, Ontario. In the United States Greyhound subsidiary Transportation Manufacturing, Inc., of Roswell, New Mexico, built the bus. A Detroit Diesel 6V-53 diesel engine was mounted in the rear.

The Indianapolis (Indiana) Public Transportation Corporation (METRO) acquired this 40-foot Orion bus, and 94 others, in 1986. This Orion was built at the Bus Industries of America factory in Oriskany, New York. METRO purchased 50 of the same Orion model in 1983. METRO opened its new operations and maintenance base in 1985. At the front of the facility is a building built in 1922 as the Duesenberg Automobile and Motors Company machine shop. The Duesenberg Company used the building until 1937. The Duesenberg automobiles built during that period were among the finest of their day. The building was completely refurbished and is currently the administrative offices of METRO.

The Urban Mass Transit Administration of the United States Department of Transportation initiated a program in 1970-71 to develop a new 40-foot standardized bus. The three major bus manufacturers, General Motors Truck and Coach Division, AM General, and Rohr Flxible, each built prototypes. The buses underwent considerable testing and were displayed in several cities. A number of features were required in the design, including a low floor. The buses were referred to as Advanced Design Buses (ADB). The program was not entirely successful. GM Truck and Coach presented the RTX bus, which lead GM to introduce its RTS bus, which had similar lines to the prototype. Although Rohr Flxible introduced an ADB bus, it was not similar to the prototype. AM General did not follow with an ADB bus and actually stopped bus production soon afterward.

The Rohr Industries Flxible bus in the Transbus program was a four-axle model with small wheels and tires, which gave it a low floor just 17 inches above the ground. A ramp was provided for access to the bus for wheelchair users. The three Rohr Flxible Transbuses received favorable reactions during public viewings. The low-floor feature may have been ahead of its time. It wasn't until the mid-1990s that low-floor buses were produced in great numbers and became industry standards.

AM General Corporation's Transbus was a three-axle bus with low-profile tires and wheels. The bus had a horizontal ramp built into the front step, but required a curb with a certain height to make it accessible for wheelchair users. The AM General bus was the weakest of the three Transbuses in the evaluation reports following public viewings in Miami, New York, Kansas City, and Seattle. None of the Transbuses were built for use in transit service, although Rohr Flxible and General Motors came out with modified Advanced Design Buses. AM General never produced an Advanced Design Bus. Bus building by AM General ended in the late 1970s.

The first transit system to operate the new GM RTS Series 01 bus was the Long Beach (California) Transportation Company. In 1977 Long Beach received 15 of the new buses. Houston (Texas) Metro Transit and VIA Metropolitan Transit of San Antonio, Texas, were also among the first systems to have the RTS buses. The 01 Series had air conditioning, but its position at the rear of the bus proved unsatisfactory, and many of the first RTS 01 buses were retrofitted to mount the air conditioning at a different location. That changed the appearance of the rear of the bus. A Detroit Diesel 6V-71 or 8V-71 engine could be chosen for this model. Long Beach Transportation Company was organized in 1963, replacing the Long Beach Motor Bus Co., which operated for a number of years.

Turbine engines for both transit and intercity application in buses were being tested and exhibited in a number of locations in the late 1970s and early 1980s. The Mass Transit Administration of Baltimore, Maryland, operated one of the 100 1978-79 General Motors RTS II buses equipped with a turbine engine. It is pictured here. At first, the turbine engine received considerable enthusiastic response, but it never went beyond the testing stage. Although there is no definite reason for its demise, the high cost of the engine was a major factor. It could use a variety of fuels, but fuel consumption was quite high. A big advantage was the low maintenance of the solid-state engine, making it a "throwaway" product after its useful life span.

The City of Whitehorse, Yukon, began Whitehorse Transit in 1974. As the bus system expanded, four 35-foot Orion buses were acquired from Calgary (Alberta) Transit in 1986 and 1987. Calgary Transit first acquired the buses in 1980 and 1982. Ontario Bus Industries in Mississauga, Ontario, built the Orion buses. These Orion buses were especially suitable to northern Canadian cities like Whitehorse, as special emphasis was given to providing good insulation, good heating, and a special front-step heater.

General Motors Truck and Coach Division of Pontiac, Michigan, produced a 60-foot articulated version of the popular RTS bus in 1980. The new bus was introduced at the International Public Transit Expo in Chicago, Illinois, that year. Articulated buses had been acquired by a number of transit systems in the United States in the five previous years. This prototype articulated bus had a Detroit Diesel 6V-92TA diesel engine mounted in the rear and an anti-jackknife system at the joint. This bus was the only General Motors articulated bus built. General Motors felt that the market for articulated buses at the time was not sufficient.

Minibus, Inc., Pico Rivera, California, began producing small buses for shuttle services, mainly in downtown sections of cities, in 1967. The Minibus pictured was operated in downtown Detroit, Michigan, by the Detroit Department of Street Railways in 1967. The standard Minibus seated 19 to 23 passengers and was powered by a Dodge engine. A dual-fuel system was available, using either diesel fuel or liquefied petroleum gas. The Minibus company built a variety of concepts for special bus transportation, including streetcar designs and bus trains especially for amusement parks.

In 1976 flamboyant John Z. DeLorean introduced a futuristic sports car, the DMC-12. It was built in Ireland. By 1983, after almost 1,000 were sold, the car-building venture closed. There was also a De-Lorean bus introduced in 1980 called the DMC-80. It was a 40-passenger model patterned after a new German design. It could be produced with a Mercedes-Benz or a MAN diesel engine. Low-profile tires allowed the bus to have a floor height 22 inches from the ground. It was not a success and none were ever sold.

This Diesel Division Model T6J4523N went into service at the Canadian Forces Station at Inuvik, Northwest Territories, in 1974. The station at Inuvik, in Canada's far north, is on the MacKenzie River Delta near the Arctic Circle. The Canadian government acquired buses for many years for service at military establishments and other locations.

Electrobus, a division of Otis Elevator Co. of Stockton, California, built a small 20-passenger battery-driven electric bus in 1974 and 1975. The Community Urban Bus Service in the Longview-Kelso, Washington, area operated one of the buses. Public bus operation got its start in the area in 1975 when the two cities purchased the Longview-Kelso Bus Company from Les Stiebritz. Transit service in the area became a Public Transportation Benefit Area in 1987. The Electrobus proved unsuccessful and only a few were ever built. A 72-pound battery was used. It was removed from the bus with a forklift and charged periodically. Another charged battery was put into the bus to continue service.

The New Orleans (Louisiana) Public Service, Inc. (NOPSI) operated streetcars throughout the city's French Quarter for many years. The Streetcar Named Desire was well known. As early as the 1930s streetcar lines were giving way to buses in New Orleans, and streetcars were gradually removed from the narrow French Quarter streets. It was decided in 1973 to use shuttle buses in the French Quarter. Eight Flxette buses were acquired for the service. These eight Flxettes were transformed in the Public Service shops to look like vintage streetcars. They were unique and served for a number of years, but buses later ran again in the French Quarter. Flxette production by The Flxible Company ended in 1975. Flxette buses were built in Evergreen, Alabama.

Kent (Ohio) State University was one of the early universities to begin a campus bus service. It began in 1967 to help relieve parking and traffic problems at the university. As the system developed, the Kent State buses were also used to provide commuter service for the university's nursing students who traveled to hospitals in Akron and Cleveland. Bus drivers, supervisors, and other employees were all students working for the bus system on a part-time basis. One of the first buses in the fleet was a GM TDH 4521, acquired in July 1968. Sixteen GM Model T6H 4523A buses were added in 1972 and 1974, one of which is pictured here. It was an air-conditioned model and featured a Detroit Diesel 6V-92 diesel engine.

Chance Manufacturing Co. of Wichita, Kansas, was a producer of high-quality amusement rides and associated equipment. The company purchased the product line of Minibus, Inc., of Downey, California, in September 1976. The Minibus RT-50 bus became the Chance RT-50 transit bus, and a new facility in Wichita was developed to build buses. The RT-50 was a small, heavy-duty bus with a Caterpillar V-8 diesel engine mounted in the front. It had seats for 25 passengers. A new concept for the RT-50 was presented a few years later. It was called the Chance Articulated Modular Transit Vehicle (AMTV), and it consisted of two passenger modules. The front was an RT-50 bus and the rear had an articulated steering system, which allowed it to track the same path as the power unit. Duke University Transit System of Durham, North Carolina, which began a campus bus system in 1977, operated several AMTV vehicles, one of which is pictured here.

Unitrans is the campus and town bus service in Davis, California, the site of the University of California at Davis. Enrollment was increasing in the late 1960s, and in 1967 two used double-deck buses were acquired from London (England) Transport. Patronage was very slow at first, but soon the double-deck buses fascinated the students and ridership grew. The double-deck fleet grew to eight vehicles by 1992, and also included a number of other buses. Maintenance of the aging double-deck buses became a challenge, but the maintenance department at Unitrans managed to keep the buses in perfect running condition, even using handmade parts fashioned by the devoted staff. The double-deck buses at Davis have become a tradition and it is possible that the original double-deck buses will serve for many more years.

The University of Connecticut in Storrs was one of many universities that established shuttle bus systems to relieve congestion and to help solve parking problems. The bus system also serviced students going to and from classes and to dormitories on the expanding campus. The service began in 1970. The first buses for the University of Connecticut were three Model T-29 Twin Coach units from Highway Products, Inc. in Kent, Ohio. Highway Products began building buses in 1968 under the Twin Coach name. Production ended in 1975 after the company had built some 900 buses.

The University of Georgia's Campus Transit System in Athens, Georgia, had its start in 1966, serving the expanding campus at the university. It was a small beginning, but by 1980 new GM RTS buses were becoming standard equipment for the Campus Transit System. Four Model T8J04 GM RTS buses went into service in 1982, one of which is pictured here. Ten more were acquired between 1983 and 1985. The buses were well liked by the students at the University, many of whom worked as bus drivers. The management also favored the buses, and RTS standardization continued. General Motors introduced the first RTS bus design in 1977. A number of changes were made to the RTS in the following years. General Motors referred to them as evolutionary changes rather than revolutionary changes.

When Albuquerque, New Mexico, formed the Albuquerque Transit System (Sun Tran), replacing the privately operated Albuquerque Bus Company, the city had a population of about 220,000. At the end of the 20th Century the population had doubled, which presented a challenge to the transit agency to provide a complete transit system. Albuquerque Bus Company, which began in 1927, also experienced considerable growth until 1965 when Sun Tran was formed. Almost without exception all buses in the fleet from 1947 to 1995 were General Motors or TMC buses. An exception came in 1978 when 24 Grumman Flxible 37-passenger Model 45096-8-1 buses were added. One of these buses is pictured here in downtown Albuquerque on the airport route.

After the oil crisis of the 1970s a number of programs for alternate fuels were proposed for use in transit buses. Bio-diesel, using soybean oil or oil from other agricultural products as an additive, was used in one of the experiments. Queen City Metro of Cincinnati, Ohio, advertised cleaner air by using soybeans as an additive to run this bus. The bus was one of 127 Flxibles purchased by Queen City Metro in 1987. These buses were actually built in 1980 and were eventually sold to the New York City Transit Authority. New York experienced failures with the engine mountings and the buses were returned to Flxible where they were rebuilt, updated, and sold to other bus systems. The Bio-diesel program has since been used in a number of cities, especially in the agricultural Midwest.

The City of Monroe, Louisiana, had transit service with streetcars dating back to the beginning of the 20th Century. Transit continued to be operated by the city, and it became known as the Monroe Transit System. Five Flxible Metro Model 35096-6T buses entered service in 1984. They were 35-foot models and seated 40 passengers. Detroit Diesel 6V-92 diesel engines powered these buses. Grumman Allied Industries, which purchased The Flxible Company in 1978 from Rohr Industries, introduced the Metro models in 1981.

The Flxible Company of Loudonville, Ohio, which had been owned by Rohr Industries, was sold to Grumman Allied Industries in 1978. A new Flxible transit bus, the Model 870 ADB (Advanced Design Bus), was announced at that time. It was an entirely new design, following the building of a prototype model under the 1971 Transbus program. Triboro Coach Corporation of Jackson Heights, New York, acquired 35 of the Model 870 Grumman Flxible buses in 1980. Triboro Coach had been a pioneer of transit service on 19 routes in the New York Borough of Queens, as well as an operator of express buses into Manhattan. Triboro Coach Co. originated in 1931, although its roots were with the Woodside-Astoria Transportation Co. from 1925.

Mississauga, Ontario, is one of the largest cities in the Toronto area. A transit system in Mississauga began in the early 1970s for urban service within the city and included routes to some outlying areas. The Ontario government conducted a three-year demonstration project to introduce articulated buses for transit in four of the largest cities in the province. Mississauga, one of the four cities, received the first 15 of the 53 articulated buses in 1982. Diesel Division of General Motors of Canada built them. Detroit Diesel 8V-71N diesel engines were mounted in the rear. To prevent jackknifing, a special turntable arrangement was incorporated. These buses had an interesting appearance with GM "New Look" bodies and a Classic Model front.

New York Bus Service of Bronx, New York, began serving the area in 1949 with local service, a sizable school bus operation, and an interesting mobile classroom service. Express bus service between Bronx and Manhattan began in 1970 with six routes. New York Bus Service had continually favored General Motors-built buses. Then, in 1984, three Classic Model buses were acquired from the Diesel Division of General Motors of Canada, including the one pictured here. They were primarily used on the express routes. New York Bus Service is a large company and has continuously operated a fleet of more than 100 buses.

Connecticut Transit (CT Transit) of Hartford, Connecticut, began a modernization program in 1990, and took delivery of 88 Motor Coach Industries Classic buses from the St. Eustache, Quebec, factory. CT Transit added 150 more of the same model Classic in 1992. These 40-foot buses had wheelchair lifts, large front entrance doors, and air conditioning. Motor Coach Industries acquired the St. Eustache plant from GM of Canada (Diesel Division) in 1987 and produced buses for many transit properties in Canada and the United States. CT Transit was formed in 1976, after taking over the services of the Connecticut Company.

Santa Monica (California) Municipal Bus Lines is one of the oldest continuously operated municipal bus systems. It began in 1928 with a single route along Pico Boulevard. There were other bus operators in the area, including Bay Cities Transit. Santa Monica Municipal Bus Lines acquired Bay Cities Transit, the largest private bus company, in 1951. The name "Big Blue Buses" was adopted and carried forward to the present day. A variety of bus makes were operated on the Big Blue Buses system, including Whites, GMs, and Flxibles. Santa Monica turned to Motor Coach Industries in 1988 and purchased 10 Model TC40102A buses. Twenty more were added the next year in two separate acquisitions. In addition to local service within Santa Monica, the Big Blue Buses continue to operate to downtown Los Angeles, Los Angeles International Airport, and to other communities.

Halifax Metro Transit became the operator of transit service in the Halifax, Nova Scotia, area in 1981. It took over the services of Halifax Transit and Dartmouth Transit. The history of transit in Halifax dates back to 1866, when the Halifax City Railroad Company began operating a horse-drawn street railway. Nova Scotia Light and Power Co. (NSL&P) was a major provider of transit service in Halifax until 1970. Trolley buses replaced streetcars in 1949, and only trolley buses were used in transit service until 1970. Buses have provided service ever since. Articulated Classic Model buses were first added to the Metro fleet in 1992, when 10 were delivered from Motor Coach Industries. Four similar articulated Model TA 50 102N buses from Nova BUS entered the Halifax fleet in 1993; the same year Motor Coach Industries sold its transit-bus building business to Nova BUS of St. Eustache, Quebec.

Appal Cart is the name of the transit system based in Boone, North Carolina. Appal Cart came into existence in 1980 under the official name, Watauga County Transportation Authority. A year later, the bus system of the Appalachian State University was merged into the system and the Appal Cart name was applied to the entire bus operation. At first school bus-type buses were used, but regular transit buses were added as the system grew. Seven 30-foot Blue Bird Q-Buses with Cummins diesel engines were eventually acquired. Four are pictured here. Blue Bird Body Co. of Fort Valley, Georgia, had been building buses since 1932. School buses were the dominant products at Blue Bird, but emphasis on transit buses increased over the years. The City Bird transit bus was introduced in 1976, and the Q-Bus was first presented in 1992.

The City of Greeley, Colorado, began operating bus service throughout Greeley and to nearby Evans in 1979. "The Bus" was the name used to market the system. Blue Bird Body Co. of Fort Valley, Georgia, delivered 13 City Bird buses to Greeley for service in 1981. The City Bird buses came in 27-foot and 31-foot lengths and were powered by Detroit Diesel 6V-71N engines mounted in the rear. The City Bird was first introduced in 1976. Blue Bird built that model for 10 years. Later, as the Blue Bird buses were being retired, Gillig buses were added to the Greeley fleet, which also includes several vans for special services.

Chapter 10

New Foreign Bus Influence

By the beginning of the 1980s local bus transportation in virtually every city in the United States was operated by a public transit agency and subsidized by the federal government and/or other government entity. The national trend was toward conservatism, with an emphasis on spending cuts and balanced budgets. There was also increased attention to human rights and environmental protection.

At the beginning of Ronald Reagan's term as president the Reagan administration was unsympathetic to transit. At one point it was suggested that the federal government discontinue subsidies to transit altogether and allow state and local governments to take over. Fortunately for the transit industry, and the population that relied on it, federal funding was continued. Several transportation

Articulated buses operated in European cities for a number of years following World War II. MAN Nutzfhrzeuge AG, an important German bus manufacturer, formed a joint venture in 1976 to manufacture articulated buses in the United States. Seattle (Washington) Metro placed an initial order for 150 of the MAN articulated buses. A consortium of 10 other transit systems followed and an order for 248 was placed. The bodies of the buses were built in Germany and finished at an AM General factory in Marshall, Texas. Pictured here is one of the 150 MAN/AM General articulated buses that Seattle Metro purchased. The articulated buses were designated Model SG 220-18-2. The buses were powered by a 220-horsepower MAN underfloor diesel engine.

acts were passed in the 1980s, mainly for the purpose of maintaining funding. Legislation passed in 1987 kept transit funding alive into the next decade.

In the 1980s ridership continued to decrease, influenced by the availability of low-cost gasoline, high unemployment figures, high interest rates, a slow economy, and inflation. These economic woes eventually improved, but many transit agencies found it necessary to increase fares to offset the increased costs. This sometimes resulted in fares of more than a dollar, a far cry from the nickel fares of the 1930s and 1940s.

In order to cut costs agencies attempted to extend the life spans of their buses by refurbishing and rebuilding older buses. This became popular and cost effective. It also spawned several new companies to fill the niche.

Dial-a-ride services, where small buses or vans picked passengers up at their doorsteps, became popular in cities in the United States and Canada.

Manufacturers continued to improve bus engines to reduce harmful emissions. There was also continued emphasis on reliability and longevity of engines and simplification of maintenance. Research continued on alternative fuels and new, more efficient, engines.

An insurance crisis occurred in 1985, which caused problems for both transit and intercity bus operations. The crisis arose from several factors affecting the insurance industry itself, not from an epidemic of bus crashes; the bus industry's safety record continued to be excellent. Instead, overall losses, natural disasters, and other forces had drained insurance resources. In 1987, as insurance rates rose dramatically, transit agencies in several states, including Pennsylvania, Wisconsin, and California, banded together to form insurance pools.

In general, federal funding had been increased to cover 80 percent of the cost of transit buses. However, in order to qualify for federal money buses had to be procured through the low-bid process. Unfortunately, by having to rely on the lowest bid, many agencies ended up with a wide variety of buses in their fleets. Mixed fleets, on the whole, tend to be more costly than a standardized fleet because of the need for a variety of parts, more training, etc. In the early days, when private ownership was the norm, mixed fleets were not commonly found. In fact, standardization of its fleet was one factor that contributed to the efficient operation and success of National City Lines.

In addition to low bids, transit systems often drove up the costs of equipment by requiring special features on their buses rather than accepting a standard model.

Following an order for MAN articulated buses from Seattle (Washington) METRO in 1978, 10 other transit systems formed a consortium to purchase 248 similar MAN buses. The buses had bodies built by MAN in Germany and were shipped to the United States for completion. AM General had the contract to finish the buses, which was done at a plant in Marshall, Texas. Phoenix (Arizona) Transit was a part of the consortium and took delivery of 20 Model SG 220 MAN/AM General 60-foot articulated buses, one of which is pictured here. In later years, near the end of the 20th Century, Phoenix invested in a large fleet of buses, ordering 303 40-foot LNG low-floor vehicles from North American Bus Industries (NABI) of Anniston, Alabama.

For instance, some specified bigger destination signs in front, changes in the windows, destination signs in the rear, or other options, all of which increased the costs.

In Canada, transit systems were experiencing many of the same problems as those in the United States, but most systems in Canada weathered the difficult times better than their American counterparts. Though transit ridership in Canada was also decreasing, the decrease wasn't as dramatic.

Both the United States and Canada had trade associations to represent transit and lead the campaign for funding. The American Transit Association and the Canadian Transit Association both adopted new names in the 1970s to better reflect changes in their membership from private to public bus systems. In 1974 the American Transit Association merged with the Institute for Rapid Transit and became known as the American

MAN Truck & Bus Corporation was established in the United States in 1980. A plant was built a few years later in Cleveland, North Carolina. MAN was known for introducing articulated buses into the United States in 1976. A new non-articulated model, the Americana, was presented in 1984. Nearly 1,000 Americana buses were built. Production of MAN articulated buses and the Americana ended in 1987 when MAN decided to discontinue building buses in the United States. Among the final Americanas delivered were 40 units that were sold to Charlotte (North Carolina) Transit System. One is pictured here in downtown Charlotte. Other Americanas went to transit systems in Minneapolis, Chicago, Seattle, and New Orleans. Charlotte Transit System became a public company in 1976, following Charlotte City Coach Company, which served from 1955. Streetcars were first seen in Charlotte in 1887, but ended service in 1938. Duke Power Company operated transit in Charlotte from 1925 to 1955.

Public Transit Association (APTA). It is now known as the American Public Transportation Association. The Canadian Transit Association had originated in 1904 as the Canadian Street Railway Association. It eventually became the Canadian Urban Transit Association (CUTA).

Commercial vehicle exhibitions, some exclusively for buses, had been staged in Europe for many decades. APTA organized the first modern-day bus exhibition in the United States in Chicago, in 1981. Known as the International Public Transit Expo, it has increased in size and in interest over the years and is held triennially. CUTA, and even state organizations, also staged exhibitions for buses.

The Union Internationale des Transports (UITP), an international association for the transit industry, held its first congress and exhibition in North America in Montreal in 1977. The association again chose North America as the site of its meeting in 1999.

Wheels is the name Norwalk (Connecticut) Transit District used to market its bus services. Due to the lack of local transit in that area, Norwalk began operations in 1978. Transportation in the Norwalk area goes back to 1862 when the Norwalk Horse Railroad Co. was formed. Scania Bussar of Katrineholm, Sweden, entered the transit market in the United States in the early 1980s. This bus had a Van Hool body on a Scania chassis and entered service in Norwalk for a short time in 1981. Scania began assembling complete buses in nearby Orange, Connecticut, in 1984.

Transit history in Madison, Wisconsin, goes back to 1884, when mules pulled trams down Madison's streets. Electrification came in 1892. The first buses came in 1924, and were operated by Wingra Bus Company. Streetcars were discontinued in 1935. The Madison Railways Co. was renamed Madison Bus Co. in 1939. Madison Metro, a public system, began in 1970. Madison Metro was one of seven U.S. and Canadian bus systems which bought buses built by Saab-Scania of America. The buses were built in a new factory in Orange, Connecticut. Madison had 24 of the Model CN 112 Scanias. Low interior noise in the Scania buses was a result of special insulation sealing the engine compartment. The buses were only built in the United States for four years. The company closed its factory in 1987.

The Volvo of America—Bus Division began building and marketing buses in 1984, using design and technology from the parent company in Sweden. A factory for the bus production was in Chesapeake, Virginia. Both 60-foot articulated and 40-foot transit buses were produced. The Southeastern Pennsylvania Transportation Authority in Philadelphia took delivery of 50 articulated Volvo buses in late 1984. Rhode Island Transit Authority of Providence, Rhode Island, San Mateo County Transit District of Burlingame, California, and New Jersey Transit of Newark, New Jersey, also had Volvo articulated buses. Within a couple of years Volvo discontinued bus manufacturing in the United States.

Volvo of America—Bus Division of Chesapeake, Virginia, began building transit buses in the United States in 1984. Both a 40-foot model and a 60-foot, articulated model were presented. All but 55 of the 230 Volvo buses built in the United States were articulated buses. Bus manufacturing was discontinued in late 1986. Three properties acquired the 60-foot articulated buses. One was the San Mateo County Transit District (SamTrans), at that time headquartered in Burlingame, California, on the peninsula south of San Francisco. SamTrans began in 1976. Thirteen of these Volvo buses were acquired in 1985—one pictured here in downtown San Francisco. Not only does SamTrans have local service on the peninsula, but it also operates service into downtown San Francisco.

The Roaring Fork Transit Agency of Aspen, Colorado, was an entirely new bus system in 1983. The growth of the winter-sports center in the late 1970s and early 1980s prompted the City of Aspen and Pitkin County officials to place a priority on a transportation system. Officials agreed it was needed to avoid gridlock produced by the many winter visitors with their own automobiles. It also needed to be "customer friendly." The result was the establishment of the new transit system. Free transportation was provided in the center area, and ski resorts contracted for the service, which proved popular to visitors. Many visitors also came in the summer, which kept the system busy year around. In 1983, 16 Neoplan Model AN 440 40-foot buses were acquired. Neoplan was a company established in Germany in 1953. When Neoplan USA was established, a new plant was built in Lamar, Colorado. *Paul Hilte*

Dallas (Texas) Area Rapid Transit (DART) has become the name of the transit system in Dallas, which became publicly owned in 1964. Dallas was growing fast and the transit system also experienced growth. An order of 30 Neoplan AN 460 articulated buses was delivered in 1986. They featured Detroit Diesel engines mounted in the rear. These buses joined Model AN 440 Neoplan buses that were in service in Dallas. Neoplan had established a new factory in Lamar, Colorado, in 1981 and began providing transit buses patterned after the buses designed by the Neoplan company in Germany.

Southern California Rapid Transit District in Los Angeles acquired 18 of these Neoplan Model N122/3 buses in 1981. These buses were an attempt to try large-capacity buses in the Los Angeles area for commuter service. Charter and tour operators also acquired the buses, known as Skyliners. Several charter and tour operators in the United States operated these models, which could seat up to 85 passengers. Power was supplied by a Detroit Diesel 8V-92TA diesel engine. Although Neoplan built buses in a new factory in Lamar, Colorado, the Skyliner was produced in the Neoplan plant in Germany.

Crown Coach Co. of Los Angeles, California, teamed with the Hungarian firm Ikarus in 1979 to market and sell 60-foot Crown/Ikarus articulated buses to transit systems in the United States. Over 200 were sold to various properties. The Milwaukee County (Wisconsin) Transit System operated 40 of these buses especially for use in Park & Ride services. Milwaukee County Transit System, a public authority, began in 1975 after many years of transit service by the Milwaukee and Suburban Transport Company.

Ottawa-Carlton (Ontario) Regional Transit Commission, also known as OC Transpo, opened an impressive Transitway system in 1983. It consisted of 8.7 miles of exclusive roadway for buses. In the beginning most of the buses used on the Transitway were Orion/Ikarus articulated models. These buses were built in Hungary and finished in Canada. They originally had Cummins underfloor diesel engines and Allison transmissions, but this proved unsatisfactory, and a Detroit Diesel underfloor diesel engine with ZF transmission was retrofitted on each bus. The first Orion/Ikarus buses were received in Ottawa in 1985. Delivery of an additional 164 buses was completed in 1988. Ontario Bus Industries of Mississauga, Ontario, manufactured, sold, and marketed the Orion/Ikarus articulated buses.

This Mercedes-Benz Model O-309 small bus operated a special service in San Bernardino, California, in the early 1970s. The service was called Omniflex. The bus was acquired by the San Bernardino Municipal Transit System, which was established in 1961. The San Bernardino Municipal Transit System succeeded the private San Bernardino Valley Transit, serving the area between 1942 and 1961. Omnitrans became the publicly owned transportation system for San Bernardino and surrounding areas in 1975 and inherited this Mercedes-Benz O-309 bus at that time. The bus was built in Germany and distributed by Mercedes-Benz of North America in Montvale, New Jersey. These Model O-309 buses saw service in a number of cities and were used for shuttle service at a variety of airports.

Westport, Connecticut, operated a small transit system in the mid-1970s. In 1977, 11 Mercedes-Benz O-309 diesel buses were in operation in Westport by the Westport Transit District. The name Minnybus became the trade name because of the small buses. Westport is near the larger city of Norwalk, Connecticut, which operates transit under the name Norwalk Transit District. The Westport system was taken over by the Norwalk Transit District in 1999. The small O-309 Mercedes-Benz buses had 4-cylinder, direct-injection diesel engines and accommodated 13 to 19 passengers. Several transit agencies throughout the United States operated these Mercedes-Benz buses.

The City Bus, built by Steyr-Daimler-Puch AG of Vienna, Austria, was introduced to the bus market in the United States in 1980. It was a small bus, seated 15 passengers, and was designed for special shuttle service. A front-wheel drive allowed for a very low floor, which was ideal for transportation of elderly and handicapped persons. A four-cylinder Daimler-Benz diesel engine mounted in the front powered the bus. Four of these buses went into service in 1980 for the County of Lebanon Transit Authority of Lebanon, Pennsylvania, which began transit service the previous year.

Ikarus USA of Moorpark, California, introduced a new transit bus in 1987 called the Model 816. The body shells for this model and other Ikarus USA models were built in Budapest, Hungary, by the Ikarus Body and Coach Building Works and were shipped to the United States for completion. The Union City (Indiana) Body Company then completed the buses. The Ikarus USA Model 436, a 60-foot articulated bus, was also offered. All models of Ikarus USA buses had Cummins or Detroit Diesel engines. This Model 816, along with seven others, was delivered to the Jacksonville (Florida) Transportation Authority in late 1989. Jacksonville Transportation Authority, a public transit system, was formed in 1971, succeeding Jacksonville Coach Co., which serviced the Jacksonville area from 1945 to 1971.

Chapter 11

Transit Reaches Out

The large number of disabled veterans returning from the war in Vietnam spurred demands by the disabled community for full accessibility to public facilities, including transit. This did not become a requirement immediately, but following the enactment of the Americans With Disabilities Act of 1990, buses had to be accessible to the disabled to qualify for federal funding.

In order to operate special transportation services for the elderly and disabled, agencies found themselves in need of vans and small buses. Many new and existing manufacturers began building small buses, many of which were lift equipped, for these special services.

Although accessibility usually meant a wheelchair lift, the need for disabled access also lead to the development of low-floor buses, which didn't require a lift to

The Gillig Phantom bus was first presented in late 1989. Three different lengths of buses were offered to transit systems and private operators: 30-foot, 35-foot, and 40-foot. The City and County of Honolulu (Hawaii) Department of Transportation Services was one of the first large transit systems to acquire 40-foot Gillig Phantom buses. Eight were delivered in 1983, followed by 24 the following year. Pictured here is one of the Gilligs in the first order on the Waikiki route. It has since been refurbished and is still operating regular service in Honolulu after more than 20 years. Honolulu is one of the many cities planning to have a Bus Rapid Transit system, which is currently needed to relieve the congestion that has become a growing problem in the Honolulu area.

Many California transit systems operate buses built by the Hayward, California, Gillig Corporation. One of these systems is the Antelope Valley Transit Authority in Lancaster. It operates urban service in Lancaster and Palmdale, as well as commuter buses to the Los Angeles and San Fernando Valley areas. The Antelope Valley Transit Authority began in 1992. Prior to that time the service was with contractors. The Authority acquired 15 40-foot Gillig Phantom buses, one of which is pictured here, in 1989. Since then more Gillig buses have been added, including 10 low-floor models.

accommodate wheelchair passengers. The first low-floor buses designed for city transit were put into service in 1990. New Flyer Industries in Winnipeg, Manitoba, manufactured them.

In addition to wheelchair accessibility, low-floor buses allowed easier entry and exit for all passengers. Because all riders were able to get on and off the bus faster, transit systems were often able to operate buses with less dwell time and, thus, a faster schedule. However, low-floor buses came with their own set of drawbacks. One major disadvantage was their diminished seating capacity. In most low-floor designs the front wheel housings were too high to accommodate seating in that location. Some low-floor buses had seating

in the rear on an elevated platform, which allowed the wheel arches to be higher, and permitted more seats in the rear of the bus. Some low-floor buses also had problems with ground clearance. In addition, many cities lacked improved bus stops that could accommodate the wheelchair ramp.

North American Bus Industries (NABI) became the new name for American Ikarus in 1996. In 1999 NABI unveiled its new CompoBus, a full-size, heavy-duty low-floor bus with a complete one-piece composite body. Because of the composite body the CompoBus was lightweight and required only two axles for its 45-foot length. In addition, the composite body was expected to be long lasting.

Trolley bus production in the United States and Canada ended in the mid-1950s, and most cities ended trolley bus service by that time or soon after. Cities such as Toronto, Ontario, decided to continue trolley bus service. In 1968, Western Flyer Coach of Winnipeg, Manitoba, built a prototype trolley bus. It was the first new trolley bus built in the United States or Canada in more than a decade. The new vehicle was shown to the Toronto (Ontario) Transit Commission, and from 1970 to 1973, 150 of these Model E700 trolley buses were delivered. Interestingly, these trolley buses used reconditioned motors from older trolley buses in the Toronto fleet. At the time the 150 trolley buses were being built, Western Flyer Coach had changed hands and was then known as Flyer Industries. Most of these trolley buses, introduced in the early 1970s, served in Toronto for 30 years. In 1993 all trolley bus service ended in Toronto.

After an absence of any new trolley bus manufacturing in the United States and Canada, Western Flyer Coach, Ltd., of Winnipeg, Manitoba, launched the new Model E700 trolley bus in the late 1960s. In 1972 the Hamilton (Ontario) Street Railway Company, which began trolley bus operations in 1950, decided to renew its fleet with the Model E700. Forty of the new trolley buses were ordered for Hamilton from Flyer Industries (the new name for the company). These buses served for 20 years, until 1992, when trolley bus service was abandoned. Motors for these trolley buses were refurbished from older trolley buses. Hamilton has a rich transit history that dates back to the time when horse-drawn streetcars operated in 1874. The Hamilton Street Railway Co. became the city's transportation provider at that time. Buses came on the scene in 1925. Canada Coach Lines of Hamilton purchased the company in 1946.

Edmonton (Alberta) Transit System began operating trolley buses in 1939. Six trolley buses from England were in the original fleet, and three more were added in 1942. During and after World War II the system expanded, and at one time there were 137 trolley buses. A new fleet of 100 trolley buses was acquired in 1980-81 to replace aging vehicles. The new trolley buses had Model T6H 5307N bodies by the Diesel Division of General Motors of Canada. These were identical to New Look GM bodies. Brown Boveri of Canada was the supplier of the electrical equipment. In recent years this fleet has been downsized to 59 vehicles. Pictured here is one of the New Look trolley buses descending the McDougall Hill near downtown Edmonton.

This GM RTS Model T7J204 of the Miami Valley Regional Transit Authority (MVRTA) of Dayton, Ohio, looks like a trolley bus with its poles extended to the trolley bus wires, but it isn't a trolley bus. It is a diesel-powered bus. The reason for the trolley bus poles is to allow this bus to follow the trolley bus lines when winter ice forms on the wires. The poles on the wire eliminate the ice. The MVRTA trolley buses can then operate with good contact from the wires. Normally this bus, delivered in 1981, operates as a regular bus on various Dayton routes. Dayton has operated trolley buses since 1933, and is the smallest city of the five in the United States that continues to operate trolley buses.

Trolley buses have been important in Vancouver, British Columbia, since 1948, when the first 82 Model T-44 CCF-Brill vehicles were delivered. The following year 86 T-48 CCF-Brill trolley buses were added. At one time Vancouver had 327 CCF-Brill trolley buses, including the last 16 that were built. Although many transit systems were eliminating their trolley bus fleets in the 1960s and 1970s, Vancouver decided to continue. Flyer Industries of Winnipeg, Manitoba, introduced the E800, E901, and E902 trolley buses in 1978 and 1982. Fifty of the Model E800s went into service in Vancouver in 1978. In 1982 and 1983, 245 of the Model E901A and E902 were delivered when the Vancouver Regional Transit System operated transit in Vancouver.

St. Catharines (Ontario) Transit Commission had its beginning in 1961. It succeeded the Niagara, St. Catharines & Toronto Railway Co., which operated urban transportation in the St. Catharines area for 60 years. The first transportation in St. Catharines was by horse railway, which began in 1879. Electric streetcars operated between 1881 and 1948. Pictured here is one of the first four Ontario Bus Industries Model 05 501 buses, which were acquired by St. Catharines Transit in 1990. Six more Model 05 501 buses were added in 1991 and five in 1992. The Ontario Bus Industries Model 05 501 bus was introduced in 1990. It became available with Detroit Diesel 6V-92 TA or Cummins L10 engines. Later, natural gas was made available for this model.

The North Slope Borough Municipal Services/Transit of Barrow, Alaska, is the northernmost urban bus system in the United States. It is situated on the Arctic Ocean. The service area is very extensive, but the main city of Barrow has the only scheduled transit service. Outlying communities have one or two buses at each location. Barrow has short summers and long winters. The buses, like this Orion V 30-foot model, are especially equipped for Alaska's cold winters. Four of these Orion V buses were acquired in 1989 to provide the main scheduled service in Barrow.

The General Motors RTS bus was one of the most popular city buses built in the United States. It was first introduced in 1977. The RTS replaced the also popular New Look transit bus. The first RTS bus was delivered, with 14 others, to Long Beach (California) Transit in 1977. It was, therefore, appropriate that the 10,000th RTS bus also went to Long Beach Transit when it was built in 1985. Long Beach operated 232 RTS buses between 1977 and 1993. Between 1990 and 1993 the Transportation Manufacturing Corporation in Roswell, New Mexico, built the Long Beach RTS buses. Prior to that time RTS buses were produced in the General Motors plant in Pontiac, Michigan. Although Long Beach did not acquire any additional RTS buses after 1993, this well-known bus continued to be built in later years by Nova BUS of St. Eustache, Quebec, which acquired the RTS bus-building operation in Roswell in 1993.

One of America's most important theme parks, Walt Disney World, opened its gates in 1970. From the beginning the park experienced widespread popularity. A transportation system operating within the theme park's boundaries has become a vital part of the large tourist area. The buses carry visitors from the entrance and parking areas to, and between, the major attractions. New General Motors RTS buses have become the backbone of the Disney World transportation fleet. The first RTS bus was delivered in 1981. By 1986 there were 53 RTS buses in service. That total grew to more than 200 buses by 2000.

Metropolitan Area Commuter System (MACS) is the name of the bus system operating in the Fairbanks, Alaska, area. MACS began in 1977, initially under a contract, but came under the jurisdiction of the Fairbanks North Star Borough in 1979. Eight 30-foot Gillig buses were acquired in 1994. During peak hours six of the buses are in service. Fairbanks has some unique operating conditions. In midwinter -70° temperatures can prevail, and in the summer temperatures can reach 90°. Because of the frequent snow and fog in the winter, strobe lights are used at the rear of the buses. Operating buses in the Fairbanks environment is a challenge, but the people who run the system make it work.

Colonial Williamsburg is a historical theme park in Virginia located at the site of the first permanent English settlement in North America. The settlement was named Jamestown in 1607 and was the nation's first capital. It was later renamed Williamsburg. Restoration of the area began in 1926, and the first site opened in 1932. After World War II the park had 11 major buildings and 17 craft shops, as well as several other attractions. A transportation system was established to transport visitors around the park. A number of GM transit buses were first used. Four Blue Bird Q buses were acquired in 1996. These buses have Cummins 5.9-liter compressed natural gas engines.

The Stewart and Stevenson Company of Houston, Texas, formed its Transit Products Division in 1989 and introduced a 40-foot transit bus known as the Apollo T-40. It was produced in cooperation with the Brazilian subsidiary of Mercedes-Benz. A Detroit Diesel V6-92 engine was mounted in the rear. Although the bus pictured here had Houston Metro transit colors, it is not known if it ever entered regular service or whether any more of this type came to the United States. The Stewart and Stevenson bus-building venture did not last.

Columbus, Indiana, the home of Cummins Engine Company, is one of the small Midwest cities that had streetcars for many years. Columbus operated a streetcar system between 1892 and 1932. Leppert Bus Lines took over the service when the streetcars were discontinued and operated local buses until 1962, when Columbus Transit was formed. It then adopted the name ColumBUS. Five Skillcraft Transmaster buses were acquired in 1987 for service in Columbus. The Transmaster was first built in 1980. Transmasters generally had 8.2-liter Detroit Diesel engines mounted in the rear. Because the entrance door was behind the front wheels, a low entrance was possible. The last Skillcraft buses were built in 1985. Approximately 115 were built in the Venice, Florida, plant.

Skillcraft Industries, Inc. of Venice, Florida, introduced a new low-floor bus in 1980. The bus normally had a seating capacity of up to 32 passengers. It was sold to many small- and medium-sized transit systems and carried the name "Transmasters." Corpus Christi (Texas) Regional Transit Authority, also known as "The B," acquired 28 Skillcraft Transmasters between 1985 and 1987. Skillcraft discontinued manufacturing buses in the late 1980s. The Corpus Christi Regional Transit Authority became a regional system in 1986. Prior to that time, Corpus Christi Transit operated the city service. Corpus Christi Transit began in 1966, replacing Nueces Transportation Company, which had operated bus service in the area for 33 years.

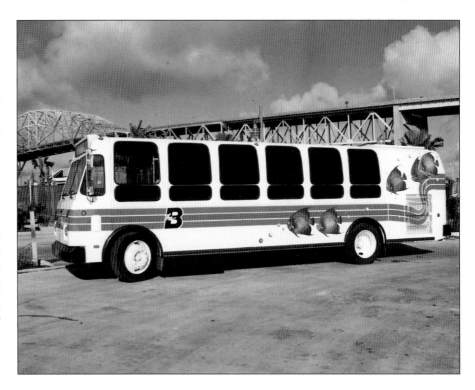

A special transportation mall was opened in downtown Denver, Colorado, in 1982. A shuttle bus service was initiated for the mall, and Minicars, Inc., of Goleta, California, built the buses chosen to operate the initial service. Thirteen diesel-powered buses with Detroit Diesel engines, and six electric buses with Westinghouse electric motors, were acquired for the one-mile route. These buses had low floors and three wide doors. They drove from the right, which provided the driver an opportunity to watch for passengers at the stops. No other buses of this type were in use elsewhere.

Advanced Vehicle Systems, Inc. (AVS), of Chattanooga, Tennessee, is a company that specializes in electric vehicles. Chattanooga Area Regional Transportation Authority (CARTA) has 17 AVS buses in downtown shuttle services. The buses use batteries, which power a Capstone Micro Turbine, a compact, lightweight turbine/generator. The maximum speed forward is 42 mph, and at a constant speed of 25 mph, the range of operation is between 45 and 65 miles. These buses entered service in Chattanooga in 1993. Transit in Chattanooga has an interesting history. The Lookout Mountain Incline Railway, the steepest in the world, opened in 1895 and continues to carry tourists and local residents today. CARTA began in 1973, succeeding Southern Coach Lines, which operated transit for 32 years.

The Super Bus was presented in 1984. It was a trailer-type bus pulled by a truck tractor. The passenger trailer accommodated 60 passengers. There was also a similar type that had two passenger trailers, each seating 29 passengers. The builders cited a number of advantages, such as the low floor and entrance, and the minimum space the mechanical vehicle took up in a maintenance facility. For a short period beginning in 1987 Orange (County) Transit District ran one of the two Super Buses between Orange County cities and downtown Los Angeles. The Super Bus was promoted into the 1990s, but the concept never attracted transit systems.

The Advanced Technology Transit Bus (ATTB) was first shown at the International Public Transit Expo in Anaheim, California, in 1996. The ATTB was designed and built by the Northrop Grumman Corporation and was the first of six prototype buses utilizing advanced technology, including epoxy ester resin to achieve light weight. Low emissions were the result of a natural gas engine using a hybrid propulsion system. This bus was advertised as "The Transit Bus of the 21st Century." The federal government funded the ATTB, and bus manufacturers were encouraged to take on the production. However, lack of funding and initiative ended the project soon after its introduction.

Greenville (North Carolina) Area Transit (GREAT) is a small transit system that began in 1976. Its fixed-route service was operated with four Thomas 31-passenger Cityliner buses which were acquired in 1991. The Cityliner bus model was first introduced in 1984. Detroit Diesel and Caterpillar diesel engines were offered. The Cityliner normally accommodated 31 passengers. Thomas has a long history of building buses, primarily school buses. Originally known as the Perley A. Thomas Car Works, the company began building streetcars in 1917 in High Point, North Carolina. Two trolley buses were also built for Greensboro, North Carolina, in 1934. Two years later school bus production began. Thomas Built Buses, which became the new name for the company when buses became a priority, is now a part of the DaimlerChrysler organization.

Soon after urban bus service was established in Klamath Falls, Oregon, in 1981, this small lift-equipped Superior bus went into operation for the new Basin Transit Service. The bus was one of the last to carry the name Superior. Superior Motor Coach Body Company was established in 1923. The name was changed to Superior Coach Corporation in 1930. Superior Coach Corporation built many school buses over a number of years. Intercity and transit buses were also built in relatively small numbers. The Sheller-Globe Company acquired the Lima, Ohio-based Superior organization in 1980. Soon after, buses were built in a plant in Morris, Manitoba, but the plant closed after only a few years. This Basin Transit Service bus was built in Morris.

The Guam Mass Transit Authority (GMTA) began in 1980. Five years later the Guam Public Transit Authority became the operator of transit on the small Pacific Ocean island. To comply with the Federal Americans With Disabilities Act (ADA), the Guam Paratransit System became operational in 1992. In 1994 the Guam Public Transit Authority and the paratransit operation operated 27 buses. All were small buses, except one 29-passenger Blue Bird. Eight of the buses, like the one pictured here, were Blue Bird Handy Buses built on Chevrolet cutaway chassis. These buses had wheelchair lifts. There were many buses of this type operating throughout the United States, mainly for paratransit service.

Carpenter Body Works of Mitchell, Indiana, began building school buses in the late 1920s. A new bus, the Carpenter CBW 300 for city transit service, was introduced in 1981. The bus was available in a 30-foot or 35-foot length and came with a rear-mounted Detroit Diesel 6V-71 diesel engine or a Caterpillar 3208 diesel. The Chicago Transit Authority purchased 20 of these 35-foot, one-door CBW 300 buses for special urban services. The Carpenter CBW-300 buses were built during a three-year period.

The Gillig Corporation introduced a 27-foot heavy-duty transit bus called the Spirit in 1989. It was powered by a Caterpillar 3208 turbocharged diesel engine. This small bus was marketed as a bus for several applications, including transit, hotel and airport shuttle, and commuter services. It was built in a plant located near the Dallas-Fort Worth (Texas) Airport. Approximately 250 were built before Gillig closed the plant and concentrated on the successful Phantom line of buses manufactured at its Hayward, California, facility. Monterey-Salinas (California) Transit and Santa Barbara (California) Municipal Transit District were two of the transit systems that operated Gillig Spirit buses.

ElDorado National Co., a Thor Industry Company in Riverside, California, is a builder of 12 bus models. Many of the buses are for paratransit use and also for shuttle services. These small buses are built on so-called cutaway truck chassis. ElDorado National resulted from a merger in 1991 of ElDorado Motor Corporation of Salina, Kansas, and National Coach Corporation of Gardena, California. The paratransit bus pictured here is an Aerotech 220 model on a Ford chassis. It has been in Dial-A-Lift service with Intercity Transit, a publicly owned bus system in Washington's state capital of Olympia. Intercity Transit was established in 1972, succeeding Olympia Transit Company, which had served the area for more than 40 years.

When the United States federal government began subsidizing public transportation, transportation for persons unable to use regular route bus service was required. As a result, fully accessible small buses were found to be the most suitable vehicles by many transit systems. Many manufacturers specializing in this type of vehicle emerged. Bodies were built on chassis built mainly by Ford and Chevrolet. These special bus chassis have been referred to as cutaway chassis. Glaval Bus of Elkhart, Indiana, is one of the manufacturers and produces several models. The Universal 25-passenger model on a Ford chassis is pictured here. It was one of 89 Universal model Glaval buses delivered to the Utah Transit Authority of Salt Lake City, Utah, in 2003. Utah Transit Authority, a transit operation since 1970, operates buses in most large Utah cities.

Chapter 12

Busways and Other Innovations

Beginning in the late 1960s a number of cities instituted Bus Rapid Transit systems to enhance bus services and help make bus travel more attractive to commuters. The first busway in the United States opened in 1969 on the Shirley Highway between Springfield, Virginia, and downtown Washington, D.C. It reduced travel time by half and attracted many commuters. The Northern Virginia Transportation Commission implemented the project.

Following the success of the Shirley Highway Bus Expressway, the 11-mile El Monte exclusive freeway right-of-way was opened in Southern California in 1973. These busways were not exclusive to buses; they were also High Occupancy Vehicle (HOV) lanes. Only vehicles carrying two or more people were allowed to use the HOV lanes.

Ottawa, Ontario's Transitways, a system of dedicated bus roadways, have been acclaimed around the world. The Transitway system first became operational in 1987 and was expanded in the years that followed. Because buses used on the Transitway can also use normal streets and roads, the buses can circulate in neighborhoods at the end of the Transitway or leave and enter the Transitway to serve neighborhoods en route. Pictured at one of the Transitway stations is one of Ottawa's 170 New Flyer Model D60LF buses, most of which are used on the Transitway. These buses were delivered to the Ottawa-Carlton Regional Transit Commission (OC Transpo) in 2001 and 2002.

The Port Authority of Allegheny County (PAT) became the operator of Pittsburgh Railways Co. in 1954. That year, it also acquired 29 independent bus companies in the Pittsburgh area. Several other private companies were later purchased. One of the most important programs of PAT was the establishment of busways. The busways are dedicated roadways, with a number of stations en route. The first was the South Busway which opened in 1977. The longer East Busway positioned alongside Conrail trackage opened in 1983. The East Busway is 6.8 miles long. Pictured at one of the East Busway stations is one of the 231 Gillig low floor buses recently added to the PAT fleet. Six of the Gillig buses are hybrid powered. PAT also operates 65 Gillig Phantom buses. The East Busway has since been expanded and a new Airport Busway in the western area has also been built. The busways were built in a short time, and ridership grew dramatically. Buses on the busways serve neighborhoods en route as well as beyond the end of the dedicated roadways.

In Pittsburgh, Pennsylvania, the Port Authority of Allegheny County (PAT) christened the exclusive South Busway in 1977. In 1983 Pittsburgh built its second exclusive busway, the 6.8-mile Martin Luther King, Jr./East Busway.

The Ottawa-Carlton (Ontario) Regional Transit Commission decided to build a busway system exclusively for buses. By the end of 1987, 12.4 miles of the new system, known as a transitway, had been completed. The transitway rapid transit system was favored because it cost 47 percent less to build than a light-rail system and cost less to operate.

Between the mid-1950s and 1980 there were only a few transit bus manufacturers in the United States and Canada. AM General, which was a division of American Motors, saw an opportunity and began building buses in 1974. Originally, Flyer Industries of Winnipeg designed the bodies. AM General's buses were built in Winnipeg, with final assembly in Mishawaka, Indiana. In the meantime, Flyer built and sold the same style bus for the Canadian market.

GM's Diesel Division in Canada began producing a newly designed transit bus in 1983 at its St-Eustache, Quebec, plant. It was called the Classic and was made available in standard and articulated models. In 1987, at the same time General Motors sold its transit bus business to Greyhound, Motor Coach Industries became the new owner of GM's Diesel Division.

One of the transit industry's most popular buses was the General Motors Truck and Coach Division RTS bus. In 1987 Greyhound Corporation purchased the bus-building business of General Motors and moved the production to Roswell, New Mexico. The RTS was then built in the factory of Transportation

Manufacturing Corporation, a Greyhound subsidiary commonly known as TMC.

The Gillig Corporation of Hayward, California, which for many years was known for its school buses, began producing transit buses. Its new model was called the Phantom and proved to be a very successful venture. Ontario Bus Industries of Mississauga, Ontario, also began building transit buses in the 1980s.

Although European-made buses had been found on the streets of American cities since the DeDion Bouton double deckers in the early 1900s, European manufacturers began to take a stronger interest in the market in the United States in the late 1970s. In 1976 Flyer Industries, which was owned by the Manitoba government, was sold to Den Oudsten NV of Woerden, Netherlands. The company became known as New Flyer Industries. The German firm MAN established the MAN Truck & Bus Corporation in the United States with a manufacturing plant in Cleveland, North Carolina.

Articulated buses had been popular in Europe for many years, but had never caught on in the United States or Canada. In 1976, Seattle Metro and a consortium of transit systems formed by the California DOT, placed orders for articulated buses. AM General and MAN Nutzfhrzeuge AG formed a joint venture to build these buses. The buses were assembled in Marshall, Texas, with the MAN body shells shipped to Texas from Germany. A number of other transit agencies also purchased articulated buses. Ikarus articulated buses, built in Hungary in conjunction with Crown Coach Corporation, were acquired by several cities.

The German manufacturer Neoplan established a plant in Lamar, Colorado, in 1981. Doing business in the United States as Neoplan USA Corporation, the company produced transit buses as well as charter and tour coaches.

Two Swedish manufacturers also entered the American bus market, Volvo and Scania. The Volvo Bus Corporation built both articulated and standard buses in a facility in Chesapeake, Virginia, until manufacturing was discontinued in 1986. Saab-Scania of America began building buses in 1986 at its plant in Orange, Connecticut. After building a small number of buses, most of which went to Honolulu, the company closed its doors in 1987.

The need for transit systems to provide lift-equipped service to the elderly and disabled contributed to the increased popularity of small buses. Small buses were also in demand for airport shuttle and even charter and tour services. Chance Manufacturing Company's Chance Coach Division, in Wichita, Kansas, introduced the small RT-50 bus in 1976. Several other manufacturers of small motor homes also began producing small buses.

School bus builders had always produced buses for the transit and intercity industry, but in small numbers. In the 1980s those numbers grew, and several school bus builders became very involved in building transit buses, particularly Blue Bird Body Co. and Thomas Built Buses. ElDorado National, which mainly built small buses, offered a full-sized transit bus in the late 1990s.

A new type of "bus" began to make an appearance on city streets. It was built to look like an old-time streetcar. Some of these vehicles were elaborately outfitted with considerable brass trim and mahogany benches and interiors. Chance Coach was one of the important builders of these nostalgic buses. Many served useful roles as shuttle vehicles in downtown circulatory services and in tourist areas.

Advertising on transit buses was not a new idea, but became more prevalent in the 1980s. Companies began specializing in selling advertising space on transit vehicles. In the very early days (1910s) car cards were mounted inside and above the windows on buses and streetcars. Some car cards are still being used today. Transit systems, seeking more revenue, began displaying ads on the sides, fronts, and backs of their buses. One of the most famous advertisements was an enlarged picture of Pepsi Cola bottle caps. The ad appeared on the fronts of buses and was seen throughout the country.

In the 2000s the latest advertising scheme was full-wrap buses. The advertising wraps around the bus, over the windows and sides. Because the advertising copy is made up of a screen arrangement, people inside the bus can still see outside, but from the outside the bus looks like a full picture.

Although private city bus systems have all but disappeared over the past 40 years, there are some new privately operated bus transportation systems. These systems have most often been operated by and/or for a particular company for its employees or tourists. Examples are the bus transportation systems at Walt Disney World in Florida and Colonial Williamsburg, Virginia. Another private bus transportation system existed in the Tri-Cities area of southeastern Washington State, providing transportation for employees on the Hanford nuclear reactor site and into nearby cities.

Seattle, Washington's central business district lies between Lake Washington on the east and Puget Sound on the west. This results in a very narrow central corridor, approximately three miles in width. To relieve congestion for transit, a 1.3-mile tunnel was built for electric trolley buses in 1990. Although Seattle had a sizable fleet of trolley buses at the time, it was decided that dual-powered buses were a good solution to the problem. Breda Construzioni Ferroviarie of Bologna, Italy, received an order from Seattle for 236 dual-powered buses. The buses were delivered in 1990-91. These buses traveled on diesel power in outlying areas and then traveled through the tunnel on electric power supplied by overhead wires. The tunnel has five convenient stations.

The Massachusetts Bay Transportation Authority (MBTA) inaugurated the Silver Line Bus Rapid Transit service in 2002. This service operates on bus-only lanes. Phase one was the first to open. Phase two to Logan Airport was the next to open. The link between New England Medical Center and South Station, which will operate in a tunnel, will open in the near future. The first Silver Line buses were 17 New Flyer 40-foot buses powered by Compressed Natural Gas (CNG). In 2004, 17 Neoplan articulated buses, as part of an order for 44, commenced service. One is pictured here. These buses are also powered by CNG. *Herb Pence*

The Alamo City Streetcar, a new and different transit vehicle, was presented by Chance Coach, Inc. of Wichita, Kansas, in the early 1980s. The design of the exterior and interior was a replica of late 19th Century streetcars. Solid mahogany was used for the seats and trim, and the spiral stanchions were solid brass. The vehicle was built on a Chance RT-50 bus and ran on rubber tires. A Caterpillar 3208 175-horsepower diesel engine was mounted in the front. VIA Metropolitan Transit of San Antonio, Texas, purchased the first 26 Alamo City Streetcars and used them on circulatory downtown routes. Tourists and San Antonioans were enthusiastic and the streetcar buses became a special attraction. Although the vehicles do not become design obsolete, VIA has retired some, and new American Heritage Streetcars have been added.

SouthWest Metro Transit of Eden Prairie, Minnesota, is one of the many transit agencies that have acquired American Heritage Streetcars from Optima Bus Corporation, formerly Chance Coach, of Wichita, Kansas. SouthWest operates two of the vehicles, the first delivered in November 2001 and the second added in June 2004. They are used for special services in Eden Prairie, Chanhassen, and Chaska, the three communities served by SouthWest Metro with urban service. Commuter routes to various destinations in the Minneapolis-St Paul area are also operated. SouthWest Metro had its start in 1983. The American Heritage Streetcars are rich in nostalgic detail, including handcrafted seats and brass rails. There are large windows and a wheelchair lift. The chassis is a heavy-duty design, and a diesel engine is mounted in the front.

The Orion II built by Bus Industries of America of Oriskany, New York, was an interesting bus, first introduced in 1984. Bus Industries of America was a part of Ontario Bus Industries of Mississauga, Ontario. The bus accommodated between 18 and 26 passengers and had a low floor, a wheelchair ramp, and front-wheel drive. These buses featured either a Cummins 48T or a Detroit Diesel 8.4-liter engine mounted in the front. Fond du Lac (Wisconsin) Area Transit acquired this Orion II and five others in 1992. Transit in Fond du Lac began in the late 19th Century with mule cars. The first bus service began operations in 1930, a year before streetcar service ended. The present city-owned transit system began in 1967, and the area transit system was established in 1978.

Double-deck buses for city transit in the United States and Canada went out of favor following World War II. With buses increasing in length and seating capacities, and the use of articulated buses, most transit agencies were able to reach an acceptable passenger-capacity level with single-deck buses. However, there was an early exception. The City of Brampton (Ontario) Transit System, which had its beginning in 1976 replacing private bus service, introduced a modern double-deck bus for transit service in early 1989. The bus was a Leyland double-deck demonstrator. It proved to be popular in Brampton, but the concept for additional double-deck buses never materialized. The Leyland Olympian accommodated 80 passengers, had two doors, and an inside stairway. *Paul Bateson*

Greenville, South Carolina, which formed the Greenville Transit Authority in 1976, took delivery of the first 15 Opus low-floor, under-35-foot transit buses from Optima Bus Corporation (formerly Chance Coach) in 2002. The buses have Cummins ISB 02 275-horsepower diesel engines and seat 31 passengers. Greenville buses operate from a large transfer center in downtown Greenville, which also houses the Greyhound bus terminal. Early transportation in Greenville was with streetcars. Trolley buses operated from 1934 to 1956, when Duke Power Company owned the system. Greenville City Coach was the transit provider from 1955 to 1976.

Knoxville (Tennessee) Area Transit operates 20 Optima Opus under-30-foot buses. Optima is the name adopted by Chance Coach, Inc. in 2002. The Opus mid-sized bus, introduced in 2000, is operated by a number of city transit fleets. Knoxville Area Transit was the name chosen by the public transit agency in 1989. The city acquired the transit system in Knoxville in 1975 and operated it under a management contract with the name Knoxville Transit Corporation. Between 1975 and 1989 the system was known as K Trans. Predecessor companies operated streetcars until 1947. There were also four trolley buses in operation for 15 years, from 1930 to 1945.

Cranbrook in Southeastern British Columbia was one of the last new transit systems in the 20th Century. Cranbrook Transit System became operational in 1999. It was part of the program by BC Transit in Victoria, British Columbia, to provide public transportation to communities throughout the province. At the time, BC Transit purchased 51 Dennis Dart 30-foot midi-buses from Dennis Specialist Vehicles in Guilford, United Kingdom. They are low-floor models equipped with Cummins diesel engines. Nine of these buses were assigned to Cranbrook Transit System to serve seven routes. Small high-headroom vans are also used in Cranbrook for a Handy DART service.

Victoria (British Columbia) Regional Transit System has 29 large-capacity double-deck buses in transit service. These buses have seating capacities of 84 passengers on two levels. The lower level is low floor, providing easy access for all passengers, including the handicapped. Dennis Specialist Vehicles of Guilford, United Kingdom, a part of Trans Bus International, built the buses. They were delivered to Victoria in 2000. Double-deck sightseeing buses have been on the scene in Victoria for many years, and have become a part of the tradition of British influence in Victoria. Cummins ISM 11 6-cylinder turbo-diesel engines are mounted in the rear of these buses. The transmission is produced by the German firm Voith. *Bill MacDonald*

Prior to World War II Anchorage, Alaska, had no transit system, although a few local intercity bus lines provided some service. Some type of urban service began in 1970 as a result of funding from the State of Alaska and the City of Anchorage. Anchorage Public Transit began in 1976. The name "People Mover" became the advertising name and was prominently displayed on most of the buses. There was quite a mixed fleet of buses in Anchorage for a number of years. The city was experiencing rapid growth, from less than 10,000 population in 1940 to more than a quarter million by the end of the century. An order for 17 New Flyer D40LF low-floor buses added to the Anchorage fleet in 1995. There was a concern about whether the low floor and low body would be a problem during heavy Alaska snows, but no problems were ever reported.

Montebello (California) Bus Lines added this Nova BUS RTS Model 06 in 1995, one of 40 RTS buses in its fleet. Montebello Bus Lines is a municipally operated transit system in the Los Angeles area, serving the City of Montebello and several other communities. It is one of several long-established municipal bus lines in Southern California. It began in 1933. Between 1928 and 1931 it was operated privately. The Nova BUS bus-building organization was established in late 1994, when it purchased factories in Roswell, New Mexico, and St. Eustache, Quebec, from Motor Coach Industries International. The RTS buses had been produced at the Roswell factory since 1987, when General Motors sold the bus-building business to Motor Coach Industries. Nova BUS continued to build RTS buses in Roswell.

The Brockton (Massachusetts) Area Transit Authority (BAT) got its start in 1968 when the Eastern Massachusetts Street Railway Company sold its large bus empire to the Massachusetts Bay Transportation Authority (MBTA) in Boston. The Brockton area was not in the MBTA area; therefore, Brockton and several other Massachusetts cities formed their own public transit systems. BAT added six Model T70 206 Nova BUS RTS buses to its fleet in February 1996 along with nine T80 206 RTS buses. Nova BUS of St. Eustache, Quebec, acquired the RTS bus-building business from Motor Coach Industries International in 1994.

Votran, the bus service of Daytona Beach and Volusia County, Florida, was formed as a public transit system in 1975. Historically, Daytona Beach had the Daytona Beach Municipal Bus Line for 30 years from 1934 to 1964. Votran has grown to become a sizable transit system, which reflects the growth of the area. It has 53 fixed-route buses and 43 paratransit vehicles. The 35-foot Nova BUS RTS bus pictured here was part of an order for 14 buses acquired in 1997. The RTS bus was introduced in 1977 by General Motors, and, with a few modifications, continued in production through the end of the 20th Century. Transportation Manufacturing Corporation took over production of RTS buses in 1988 and Nova BUS in 1994.

Monterey-Salinas Transit serves both Monterey and Salinas, California, as well as a number of other cities on the Monterey Peninsula and in Monterey County. The area has a notable transit history dating back to 1893. The predecessor transit provider to the publicly owned system was Bay Rapid Transit, which served for more than 50 years. Monterey Peninsula Transit came into existence in 1973, and in 1981 merged with the Salinas Transit System to become Monterey-Salinas Transit. A variety of bus types have served the area over the years. The newest buses are from the Gillig Corporation. Pictured with a beautiful Pacific Ocean background is one of the 24 low-floor Gillig buses. Monterey-Salinas Transit also operates eight 35-foot Gillig Phantom and eight 40-foot Gillig Phantom buses. *Monterey-Salinas Transit*

Urban transportation in Quebec City has a long history that began in 1899. At that time, Quebec Light & Power Company operated the transit service. Quebec Autobus was the transit operator from 1957 to 1970. A series of municipal organizations followed, and now service is operated by Reseau de Transaport de la Capitale (RTC). Nova BUS of St. Eustache, Quebec, presented its low-floor Model LFS bus in 1994. Quebec City acquired 10 of the new models soon afterward. By the end of the century there were nearly 100 of these buses in the fleet. Pictured here, having just passed through St. Louis Gate on a snowy day, is one of the Nova BUS buses delivered to Quebec in 2000.

Niagara Frontier Transportation Authority of Buffalo, New York, took delivery of 21 Nova BUS Model LFS 40-foot buses in 2000. The Nova BUS LFS model was first introduced in 1994 and has since been acquired by a number of transit systems in the United States and Canada. LFS models feature a Cummins 8.3-diesel engine mounted in the left rear corner. The low floor extends through the length of the bus. A Detroit Diesel Series 40 engine is an option. The Niagara Frontier Transportation Authority became a public system in 1968, succeeding the Niagara Frontier Transit System. This system serves Buffalo, Niagara Falls, and a large area of Western New York with transit service.

City bus systems had always sold advertising in and on buses. First, advertising was only inside the bus, but outside advertising became common in the 1950s. Beginning in the 1990s, advertising called wraps, covering the entire sides of a bus, was introduced. Pictured is a Gillig Phantom bus of the Central Florida Transportation Authority (LYNX) of the Orlando, Florida, area. LYNX has acquired more than 200 Gillig Phantom buses. Those buses not carrying wrap advertising for LYNX are in different colors. Transit began in Orlando in 1881 and privately operated until 1972 when the public system began.

Chapter 13

Federal Funding Increases; Technology Improves

In the 1970s the Detroit Diesel and Allison divisions of General Motors merged to form the Detroit Diesel Allison Division. In 1974 the Detroit Diesel Allison Division began production of its 92 Series two-cycle diesel engine. Detroit Diesel Allison Division introduced Detroit Diesel Electronic Controls (DDEC) for its diesel engines in 1985. The company also introduced a new four-cycle heavy-duty diesel engine, known as the Series 50, to the transit bus market in 1993. The larger Series 60 was later introduced.

In 1995 Cummins Engine Company began offering its new M-11E engine, a four-cycle diesel engine that succeeded the popular L-10. The L-10, which had been introduced in 1985, was a four-cycle, turbocharged engine for large buses. Many transit systems had ordered new buses with the L-10 engine. Cummins diesel engines

King County Department of Transportation of Seattle, Washington, replaced aging AM General trolley buses in 2001, acquiring a fleet of new trolley buses using Gillig 40-foot bodies. Electric motors used in the buses came from the 100 AM General trolley buses that were replaced. The Alstrom Transportation Company refurbished the motors. A similar arrangement occurred 30 years previously when older trolley buses in Toronto and Hamilton, Ontario, were replaced by new-bodied trolley buses with refurbished motors from the vehicles replaced. Seattle has been operating trolley buses continuously since 1940.

Dayton, Ohio, has had trolley buses in service on its streets since 1933. During the 1930s there were five separate trolley bus companies in the Dayton area. Mergers took place, and City Transit Company became the single transit system in 1955. Miami Valley Regional Transit Authority (MVRTA), a public company, was formed in 1973. Trolley bus service continued. As fleets of trolley buses aged, new and even used trolley buses were acquired. In the early 1990s a search was underway for new trolley buses. A joint venture of Electric Transit, Inc., which had been formed by AAI, a subsidiary of United Industrial Corporation, and Skoda Ostrov sro, a Czech Republic firm, submitted a proposal for new trolley buses in Dayton. The MVRTA placed an order for 57 new trolley buses. The first three came in 1996 and the remainder in 1998. The new vehicles are Model 14TREs, one of which is pictured here.

were also very popular for small buses. Cummins had produced four-cycle engines for many years, but the company became more involved in supplying engines for buses in the 1990s. Caterpillar, Inc. also offered diesel engines to the bus industry.

Clean air was still a major concern, and engine manufacturers continued to improve engines to reduce the amount of harmful emissions. The state of California implemented very strict emissions requirements. Its program for improving engine emissions made it a leader in that regard. Many methods for reducing emissions were considered and implemented, including upgraded electronic systems, "clean diesel" fuel, catalytic converters, and alternative fuels. Hybrid buses, utilizing a combination of diesel or gasoline and electric power, were produced, and fuel cell

experiments began to show promise as the propulsion systems of the future.

In 1990 Seattle Metro completed a transit tunnel beneath the city's downtown streets. A fleet of new articulated, dual-powered trolleys was acquired for service in the tunnel and on city streets. Breda Construzioni Ferroviarie in Italy supplied these. In addition, 100 New Flyer buses equipped with Allison hybrid electric drive were introduced for service in Seattle. The hybrid buses were powerful enough to climb the Seattle hills efficiently, and because of the low pollution they produce, could be operated in the downtown tunnel.

Both Detroit Diesel and Cummins had begun offering alternative-fuel engines, particularly natural gas, to customers specifying them. Detroit Diesel initially had a methanol fuel program, but later worked on natural gas installations. Early programs from Cummins involved compressed natural gas and liquefied natural gas.

Natural gas had been in use for a number of years for city transit buses. Although natural gas engines emit fewer pollutants than diesel engines, the technology comes with a high infrastructure cost. With the continued improvements in diesel engine technology, and with hybrid buses becoming more practical and affordable, some transit agencies chose not to make the investment in natural gas, opting instead to wait for the newer technologies.

Bus technology continued to improve. Multiplex and other improved wiring systems, air conditioning, automatic transmissions, tires, paint, brakes, and other components were continually being upgraded. Air conditioning systems became more challenging after the government ruled CFC-based refrigerants had to be phased out.

Bus safety, which had always been excellent, was further improved by the passing of the Commercial Drivers License and Motor Carrier Safety laws.

Electric buses began to appear. Electric battery-powered buses had been operated in the past, albeit with little success. Newer projects showed more promise. Battery buses began operating in Chattanooga, Tennessee, and Santa Barbara, California.

Funding for transit continued to be a concern, particularly as costs continued to rise. The Americans With Disabilities Act of 1990 and the Clean Air Act both contributed to the rise in equipment costs.

Federal funding received a boost with the passage of the Intermodal Surface Transportation Efficiency Act (ISTEA) in 1991. ISTEA provided funding through March 31, 1998. This act was flexible, in that it allowed funds to be used for either highways or transit; whichever was most suitable for specific local areas. Federal fuel taxes dedicated for transit were increased by one or more cents per gallon. ISTEA also included $200 million a year for rural intercity bus service and had a provision for adding High Occupancy Vehicle (HOV) lanes in a number of metropolitan areas. HOV lanes gave transit systems an opportunity to implement their Bus Rapid Transit, speeding services to city centers.

In 1998 another new funding bill was enacted. The Transportation Equity Act for the 21st Century (TEA-21) provided dedicated transit funding for a six-year period. As a result, funding for transit increased by 40 percent. Funding under this bill was also flexible between highways and transit, and rural transportation programs were included as well.

During the 1990s foreign management companies and consolidations sprang up. Coach USA was one of the first of the modern bus company consolidations. Although Coach USA involved mostly intercity and sightseeing companies, it did have some transit bus operations. Later, Stagecoach of Scotland purchased Coach USA.

First Bus in England purchased ATE Management Co. and operated some transit service. In addition, France's Conex and others also became involved with transit contracts.

The San Francisco (California) Municipal Railway (MUNI) continues to have a sizable fleet of approximately 350 trolley buses. In the 1990s replacement of older trolley buses, mostly built by Flyer Industries, became a necessity. After considerable discussion it was decided to solicit bids for new trolley buses. Electric Transit, Inc. (ETI), which had an arrangement with Skoda Ostrov sro, was the successful bidder for the new MUNI trolley buses. The bid was for 220 two-axle trolley buses and 30 articulated three-axle trolley buses. Twenty more two-axle trolley buses were added a short time later. Skoda Ostrov was a leading producer of trolley buses, especially after World War II. Most of the 12,289 trolley buses produced went to Eastern European transit systems. The Skoda Ostrov factory in the Czech Republic closed its doors following the San Francisco delivery. Pictured here is one of the ETI/Skoda articulated trolley buses in downtown San Francisco.

When the federal government enacted legislation for the funding of buses, it agreed to subsidize the purchase of buses by 80 percent. That ruling included a strong provision requiring that a certain amount of the buses had to be built in the United States. In the 1980s, as more European manufacturers decided to begin building buses for the United States market, they established factories in the United States. Although bodies or other parts of the buses were built overseas, a certain amount of American product was required in the buses. In more recent times buses acquired by transit systems in the United States have been completely or partially built in Europe. Because no manufacturer in the United States would build a particular bus that was required by a transit system, a waiver from the Buy America provision was allowed. This was true of the NABI CompoBus, built mainly in Hungary.

Citizens Area Transit in Las Vegas purchased 10 articulated tram-like vehicles from Irisbus in France. Alameda Contra-Costa Transit in Oakland, California, purchased 134 A330 single-deck buses and 57 AG300 articulated buses built in Belgium by Van Hool. ABC Bus, which markets Van Hool intercity tour and charter buses in the United States, participated in this acquisition.

In 1999 several communities were selected to take part in federal Bus Rapid Transit (BRT) demonstration projects. The goal of BRT planning and technology was to allow agencies to operate buses with the speed and efficiency of light-rail vehicles at a fraction of the cost. Cleveland, Ohio, Honolulu, Hawaii, and Eugene, Oregon, were cities that implemented BRT systems.

The Massachusetts Bay Transportation Authority (MBTA) of Boston, Massachusetts, began taking delivery of 32 new low-floor trolley buses in 2004. The trolley buses were jointly produced by the German firm Neoplan and the Czech Republic firm Skoda. Trolley buses in Boston had left-hand doors because passengers left the trolley buses on the left side when they transferred to subway trains in a tunnel. The Boston Elevated Railway, predecessor to the MBTA, operated a fleet of 463 trolley buses in 1950. Most of the trolley buses were built by the Pullman-Standard Car Manufacturing Co. at its Worcester, Massachusetts, factory. The trolley bus system in Boston was considerably downsized, and in 1976, only 50 Flyer Industries trolley buses were required for the service. It is expected that trolley bus service will continue in Boston for the foreseeable future. *Herb Pence*

Pierce Transit of Tacoma, Washington, was one of the first transit systems to use compressed natural gas (CNG) as an alternative fuel for buses in its fleet. Two 1974 "New Look" GM buses were converted to use CNG in 1986, and after evaluation it was decided CNG was the future for Pierce Transit. Pictured is one of the 44 New Flyer Model C40LF 40-foot low-floor buses added to the fleet beginning in 1998. Twenty more were later added. Almost all Pierce County buses are low floor or lift equipped and powered by CNG. Transit first operated in Tacoma in 1888. Tacoma Railway and Power was the primary provider of transit until 1941, when Tacoma Transit began. Although transit in Tacoma became a public system in 1961, the present Pierce Transit, a county system, was formed in 1979.

Blacksburg, Virginia, a college city in Western Virginia where Virginia Polytechnic Institute and Virginia Tech are located, was finding a need for a transit system in 1983. That is when Blacksburg Transit began serving the city and colleges. Its first buses were eight 30-foot Blue Bird City Bird buses. The system soon outgrew those buses and new, larger buses were acquired in 1986. New Flyer buses were added to the fleet in 1998. Pictured here is one of the nine D35LF 35-foot low-floor models currently in service. Blacksburg Transit also operates five 1998 30-foot New Flyer buses.

The Milwaukee County (Wisconsin) Transit System has been a good customer for buses from New Flyer Industries of Winnipeg, Manitoba, for several years. More than 300 low-floor New Flyer buses are in service, mainly D40LF models. Twenty of the smaller New Flyer Model D30LF buses were added to the Milwaukee fleet in 2002. New Flyer became the first North American bus manufacturer with a new low-floor model bus, first introduced in 1989. Many transit properties throughout the United States and Canada are now operating low-floor New Flyer buses. Four different low-floor models have been offered. The Model D30LF pictured here is popular in small cities, but some cities, like Milwaukee, find the bus useful for certain services.

Bettendorf, Iowa, is a growing city at the edge of Davenport. The city opted to have its own bus service and began a transit system in 1974. The system started with a number of light-duty cutaways and other small buses. The fleet was upgraded in 2004 with six KM 1030 buses sold by ABC Companies in Faribault, Minnesota. The buses are built on Freightliner FB 65 chassis and have Cummins ISB 205-horsepower diesel engines in the front. The Bettendorf buses feature air conditioning, wheelchair lifts, and seating for 27 passengers.

The first transit buses built by Gillig were 35 feet long, but soon 40-foot and 30-foot lengths were added. Many transit systems ordered the heavy-duty Gillig buses. Recently, a new low-floor small bus has been offered by Gillig, but in less than a 30-foot length (actually referred to as a 29-foot model). One of the transit systems operating the 29-foot Gillig low-floor buses is the Sioux Falls (South Dakota) Transit System. Currently, Sioux Falls has eight in service. One is pictured here in front of the system's new downtown transfer station. Sioux Falls Transit also operates 17 30-foot Gillig Phantom buses.

Chapter 14

Street Ahead

Transit has become a part of government activity and, to some extent, a social necessity. Funding has become a major political concern. Because of the many governmental regulations and restrictions, it sometimes takes longer than it should for issues to be addressed and to implement new and improved transit projects. The debates over transit have resulted in delays in adopting new programs, while at the same time accelerating other programs before they had been thoroughly tested or found to be a necessity.

Making transit more available and more acceptable to the public will continue to be a major focus for transit systems, transit associations, and government at all levels. Transit systems around the country, as well as the national and regional transit associations, will

CompoBus is the name of the composite-bodied transit bus first shown in 1999 at the Union International Transport Publics (UITP) Congress in Toronto, Ontario. It is a product of North American Bus Industries (NABI) of Anniston, Alabama. The bodies of the CompoBus are made of glass-fiber, vinyl-ester resin laminate resulting in a lightweight one-piece body. The first deliveries of the CompoBus to a transit property in the United States were to the Phoenix (Arizona) Valley Metro system in 2002. The 56 new CompoBuses were assigned to a new Bus Rapid Transit (BRT) service called RAPID, which operates during morning and evening commuter times between Park & Ride lots and other locations, and downtown Phoenix. The CompoBuses lightweight construction allows them to be 45 feet in length with two axles. Liquefied natural gas engines are used.

continue to promote the importance of transit, not only to those who have come to rely on its services, such as the handicapped, the elderly, and children, but also to society in general due to its role in relieving congestion and air pollution.

The remarkable experience of safety in bus transportation is very important, and the industry should be commended for its record of safe service. New technology is making buses for urban transit safer, more efficient, and more convenient for the passenger. Most cities now have buses that are 100 percent accessible. Low-floor buses, which were introduced in the 1990s, have been a great help to elderly and handicapped riders, and have made it easier for everyone to get on and off the buses.

New technology for 21st Century buses has been quite dramatic. Alternative fuels are powering buses in a number of cities. Natural gas is the most common alternative fuel, but others are also being used. Hybrid buses, using a combination of a diesel engine, batteries, and an electric motor, are in service in a number of cities across the United States. These include Seattle, Washington, which has 100 new hybrid articulated vehicles, and Minneapolis and St. Paul, Minnesota, where hybrid buses have operated in regular service for the past few years. Fuel cell technology is also being tested in several cities. Fuel cell engines and the hydrogen fuel they use are very expensive; therefore, fuel cell engines are not as promising for the future as hybrid technology is.

In the past decade there has been considerable emphasis on Bus Rapid Transit and busways, and certainly that will continue to be an important focus for the future. Busways offer a great potential because they can speed up transportation considerably and be very cost effective. Busways have a number of advantages over light- or heavy-rail systems. They offer considerable flexibility transporting people on the busway and then on local streets, both in outlying areas and in downtown areas. Busways can provide service to intermediate areas by allowing the buses to operate part way on the busway and then exit the busway and serve different neighbor-

hoods. Busways also allow the buses to be serviced and maintained in present maintenance facilities. In most cases, new maintenance facilities are not required.

Transit systems with Bus Rapid Transit or busway programs are requiring more attractive and different-looking buses. Manufacturers are responding with new designs. Most of these new buses are articulated vehicles and can accommodate a large number of passengers. In some foreign cities bi-articulated buses, seating as many as 200 people, are in service on busway systems, and these buses may be introduced in the United States in the near future. Not only can articulated or bi-articulated buses operate on busways, they can also operate just as easily as normal buses on city streets.

In recent years government agencies responsible for the funding of transit have attempted to economize, and taxpayers have resisted efforts to increase taxes. Therefore, transit agencies have had considerable problems getting enough funding to operate their systems. This has required the agencies to look for ways to increase revenue or save on expenses. Advertising offers one way to increase revenue. This not only includes ads on the buses themselves, but also on timetables, shelters, and benches. One unique method for saving on expenses has been showing up at a number of agencies. It results from a clause in some driver contracts, which allows agencies to pay drivers a lower pay scale if the buses they drive are less than 30 feet long. Agencies have been purchasing heavy-duty small buses that are designated as 29-foot buses, even though some are just inches from the 30-foot mark. By doing so they are able to pay drivers the lower scale and save money on wages.

Businesses in many communities are recognizing the importance of transit and have begun subsidizing the commute of many of their employees. Making subsidies available to employees is helping reduce traffic congestion and pollution in a number of cities.

No doubt the high cost of energy is going to continue for many years and that should also have an impact on making transit more affordable and more attractive to riders.

Hybrid-powered buses had been talked about for the future in bus transportation throughout the last years of the 20th Century. The first large order for 212 hybrid buses came from King County Metro Transit, which operates transit service in the Seattle, Washington, area. The new hybrid buses are built by New Flyer Industries of Winnipeg, Manitoba. The buses are Model DE60LFs and are identical to other low-floor articulated buses, which have been on Seattle streets since 1998. However, on the newer New Flyer buses the propulsion is different. Caterpillar diesel engines and Allison electric drive units are being used. Because the new hybrid buses emit a minimum of pollutants, they can operate through the downtown Seattle transit tunnel, where only electric trolley buses could operate previously. Although the hybrid buses are expensive, it is expected the price for each bus will be reduced as more come into service.

The world's first parallel hybrid bus was built by the Gillig Corporation in 2000. The first three went into service in October 2002 on the streets of Minneapolis and St. Paul, Minnesota. The Metropolitan Transportation Commission, which serves the area, acquired these three buses. They have Cummins diesel engines and Allison electric drives. The drive is in a parallel configuration, which means it can blend electrical and mechanical power to drive the wheels to get higher efficiency and better performance. At  lower speeds the electrical motor is more efficient, but at higher speeds the diesel engine is better, so the electronic "brain" selects the best power source to get an optimum blend. Batteries in the bus store recaptured braking energy which is reused later, thus further saving energy and fuel. The Metropolitan Transportation Commission first began operating Gillig buses in 1989, when 125 40-foot models were acquired. Since then more than 850 Gilligs have been delivered for operation in the Minneapolis-St. Paul area.

St. John (New Brunswick) Transit Commission has the distinction of operating with 65 percent of its revenue coming from fare box revenues and the remainder from subsidies. The Commission was formed in 1977, acquiring the transit system from City Transit, Ltd. Two Orion VII buses were purchased in 2003. One is pictured here. Ontario Bus Industries of Mississauga, Ontario, introduced the low-floor Orion VII model in 2003. Ontario Bus Industries, which began marketing buses in 1976, is one of several companies owned by DaimlerChrysler Commercial Buses of North America.

New buses, such as the Van Hool low-floor bus pictured here, have been a part of the program to enhance bus riding by Alameda Contra-Costa Transit (AC Transit) of Oakland, California. There are 134 of these Van Hool buses assigned to the RAPID service introduced in 2003. In addition to the new buses, there has been a simplified plan to introduce the Bus Rapid Transit, which features fewer stops with special street side stations, progressive traffic signals, and stops at the far sides of intersections. This resulted in faster bus service and increased ridership during the first year. One of the busy corridors, the 16-mile San Pablo route, is the first for the new RAPID service. Because of its success other RAPID routes are planned. The Van Hool buses, manufactured in Belgium, were chosen because of their flat floor throughout the bus and three doors for speedier passenger movement. ABC Bus of Faribault, Minnesota, is the distributor and representative for Van Hool buses in the United States. AC Transit also has taken delivery of 57 articulated Van Hool buses.

Ten futuristic articulated transit vehicles called Civis began operating a special Bus Rapid Transit service in Las Vegas, Nevada, in 2004. The vehicles, one of which is pictured here, are built in France by Irisbus, one of the largest bus manufacturers in Europe. The Civis are optically guided by markings in the busway. This allows the Civis to accurately come to the curb at each of the 20 stations on the route. The MAX route, as it is called, is one of the busiest routes of Citizens Area Transit, the operator of transit in Las Vegas. The 13-mile route takes 28 minutes in each direction, compared to 47 minutes with the previous bus service. The Regional Transportation Commission of Southern Nevada, which overseas transportation in the area, has established a monorail route and is considering double-deck buses on another busy route. Transit in Las Vegas is busy 24 hours a day due to the 24-hour activity at Vegas casinos. Interestingly, Las Vegas had one of the last private bus systems in the United States. The private Vegas Transit Lines gave way to Citizens Area Transit in 1983.

The Inverio® is New Flyer Industry's new bus for transit's future. It was first presented in 2002. The first large order for this new model, the D401, came from the Ottawa-Carlton (Ontario) Regional Transit Commission (OC Transpo). The initial delivery of 73 Inverio buses for Ottawa began in December 2003. A total of 294 of these new buses will be delivered. They are low-floor models, but unlike previous New Flyer low-floor buses, they seat 41 passengers instead of 39 passengers. The heating and air conditioning unit is located on the roof in the front. OC Transpo also has New Flyer 60-foot articulated buses in service. They are currently used along with the newer buses on the leading Transitway routes in the Ottawa area.

North American Bus Industries (NABI) of Anniston, Alabama, has been an important supplier of buses for the Los Angeles (California) Metropolitan Transportation Authority (LACMTA). Many of the 875 compressed natural gas (CNG) buses in the LACMTA fleet are used on three new Bus Rapid Transit routes. The routes operate along important corridor streets with limited stops and priority signals. Service is very frequent, and the response to the RAPID, as the service is called, has been very rewarding. LACMTA is planning more Bus Rapid Transit routes. The most recent order for NABI buses was for 200, 60-foot CNG 60-BRT articulated vehicles, one of which is pictured here, and 100, 45-foot CNG CompoBuses.

The Sierra Spirit is a special free circulatory bus service in downtown Reno, Nevada. Regional Transportation Commission (RTC) of Reno and Washoe County purchased four under-30-foot, mid-sized buses from Optima Bus Corporation for this service in 2003. The buses are bright yellow in color and have attractive graphics. Tourists and downtown workers are welcomed to use the free buses, which also serve the University of Nevada. RTC began operating bus service in the Reno area in 1978, replacing a small bus system known as Reno Bus Lines, Inc. RTC contracts the operation of the city service and the Sierra Spirit under the name of Citifare. Reno operated streetcars in the early days, but they were discontinued in 1927, when Reno had a population of just 10,000.

Index

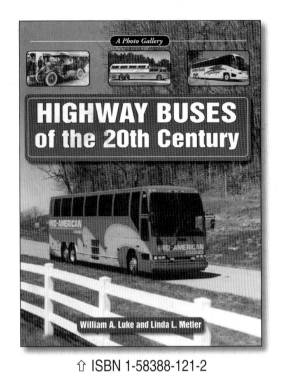
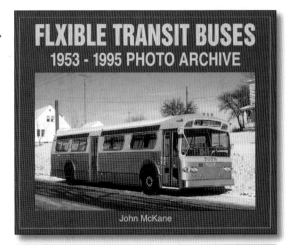
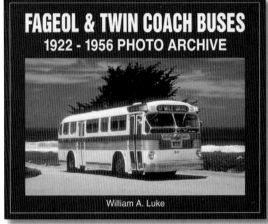
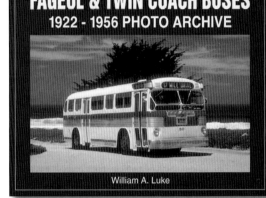

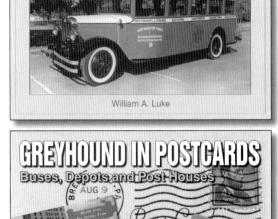
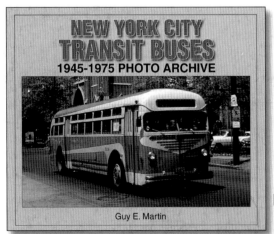